CERTIFY Associates

Disruption!

23 Immutable Truths

Your business will face disruptions.
They can appear from anywhere at any time.
Are you prepared?

ISBN: 979-8-9899555-7-2

Disruption: 23 Immutable Truths

Prologue

The epidemic of 2020 brought levels of business disruption unlike anything prior. Most companies experienced enormous operational challenges. Hospitality, personal services, movie theaters, food services, and even healthcare saw tremendous operational declines. Consider these U.S. statistics: during COVID, 59% of hotels faced foreclosure, one hundred thousand restaurants closed, and healthcare saw a 300+ billion-dollar loss. Movie theaters faced a double whammy in that the epidemic disruption also led to changes in consumer preferences as home streaming increased by over 44 percent.

Many hard-hit sectors responded with new models: outdoor exercising for local gyms and home delivery for restaurant orders. How does an organization gain resilience for the next significant disruption (and there will be many more!)? Business leaders must understand potential vulnerabilities and create abilities to mitigate or compensate for them. This book helps leaders start reflecting on their operations and preparing for upcoming disruptions that may occur tomorrow or a decade from tomorrow. In the process of reflection, they might find a way to bring their own innovative disruption to the market.

The book is divided into 23 sectors of disruptions (each one originally a white paper), across seven categories: Technology, Competition, Personnel, Operations, Customer, External, and Two to Grow On! We label the sectors "immutable" 1) to reflect that disruptions indeed will occur and 2) to pay homage to our favorite business book, The 22 Immutable Laws of Marketing (Al Ries and Jack Trout, HarperCollins Publishers, Copyright © 1993).

Regarding technology transformation, will you be a disruptor or disruptee? Being the disruptor (offense) offers you a technology lead and first-mover advantage. If you are not the disruptor, you are the disruptee, which means that you will soon experience an industry shift and be at the mercy of the disruptors' efforts to acquire customers. Of course, disruption can result from much more than competitors' efforts. We have tried to cover the gambit of disruption in this compilation. You will find that the arrows of disruption can come from all angles!

Table of Contents

Introduction

Background & Introduction. Disruption to your business can occur at any time. The disruption could be a weather event. It could be a geopolitical event. It could be a technological advancement. Let's start with technology. Every business is challenged to address the disruption caused by new technologies. The skills, tools, and know-how in the pipeline (here today) are daunting. The instruments that you use to operate your business are obsolete almost before you take delivery. On the horizon today are 5G, 6G, enhanced RFID, enriched IoT, 3D printing, robotics, drones, greater data storage, and faster speeds for everything.

Some businesses have thrived as they already had an agile business model that could cope seamlessly with heightened technology disruption. You can prepare yourself, confidently catch up, and get ahead of your competition by building disruption into your business strategy. The solution is not complicated; it's transformative. See Figure 1.

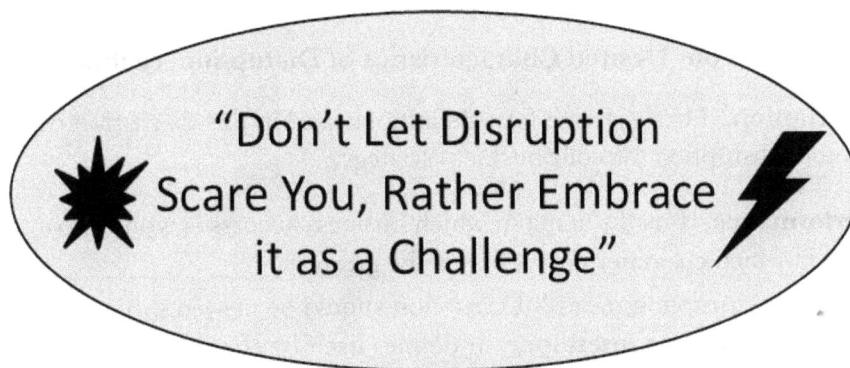

Figure 1: Embrace Disruption as an Innovation

What does innovative disruption mean, and how do I insert it into my business paradigm? Is my business (leadership, personnel, apparatus, and suppliers) ready for the necessary transformation? Let's use an example to illustrate our point. As our example, we will highlight a scenario utilizing digital disruptive technology related to the supply chain. This is just an example, albeit an important one. However, we could use an interloper disruption, such as a hurricane or pandemic, just as well.

Purpose. We will aim high and define our no-touch supply chain goals as follows. To illustrate how disruption can be an innovator, we will use a no-touch supply chain as an example.

Challenge. We will utilize today's new technologies to automate our product flow from supplier to customer as much as possible. See below for the next level of details on our challenge.

- Improve supply chain Performance, Availability, and Supportability.
- Realize a reduction in overall operating and support costs from manufacturer to user.
- Experience a return on investment in months. Supports risk management of products, workers, transportation, and customers.
- Improve operator performance by providing feedback at each point of performance.

- Reduce the number of repetitive maintenance tasks.
- Reduce carbon footprint.
- Reduce liability protection costs, insurance claims, and unnecessary litigation.

Description. The goals listed above are ambitious but achievable, and best of all, they can be accomplished using no-touch warehouse technologies that enjoy the following four characteristics, as shown in Figure 2.

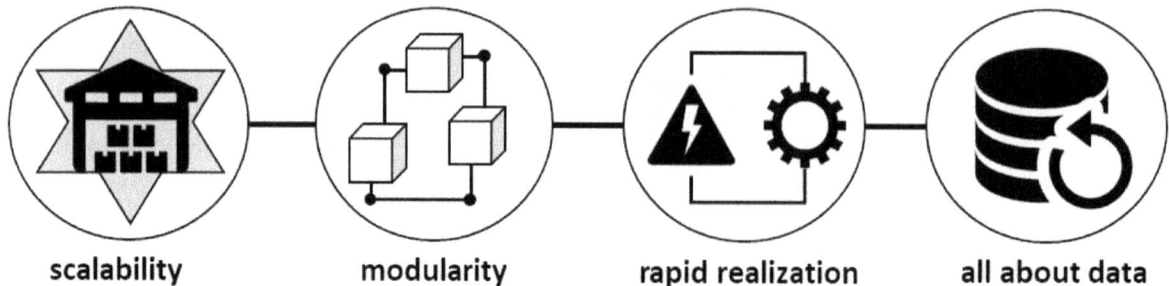

| scalability | modularity | rapid realization | all about data |

Figure 2: Four Desired Characteristics of Disruption Technologies

Understand Disruption. Let's examine four definitions used in this discussion of leveraging technology to embed disruption into our business strategy.

- **Point of Performance.** It is the arena in which business success is won or lost. It is the highest profile setting in which customer interaction is the greatest.
- **Disruption.** What disruption means! Disruption should be viewed through at least three lenses. First, disruption is an **interloper**. It defines itself by altering the business environment (e.g., climate, pandemic, government regulation, etc.). Second, disruption is an **innovator**. It incorporates new technology (e.g., IoT, AI, 5G, RFID, etc.) into the business processes. Third, disruption is an **opportunity**. It leverages disruptive events (e.g., tax breaks, earthquakes, labor strikes, 3D printing, etc.) into a successful business enterprise.
- **Digital Transformation.** Digital transformation integrates **digital technology** into all business areas, fundamentally changing how the company operates and delivers value to its customers. It's also a **business cultural change** that requires organizations to continually challenge the status quo, experiment, and get comfortable with disruption (interloper, innovator, and/or opportunity).
- **No-Touch Supply Chain.** The practice of managing assets to achieve optimized sustainment performance at an affordable cost while **meeting demand objectives**, minimizing the handling of the transportation and distribution of as many supply chain tasks as possible.

Measure Success. We need agreement on our desired outcome from all stakeholders – write it down! Now, determine how we know we succeeded by settling on the performance measurement. There are several ways to quantify success: profits, litigations, time to fulfillment, customer satisfaction, safety, etc. See Figure 3 for significant elements of the supply chain.

Now, let's examine the methodology. First, what features do we seek, and what questions do we ask ourselves? The no-touch supply chain aims to achieve the following features.

1. Algorithms to optimize sustainment tasks
2. Low-cost but reliable communications for data capture & transmission
3. Flexible architecture designed to integrate emerging technology
4. Innovative techniques for Point of Performance support tools
5. Modeling & Simulation used to reduce troubleshooting time and increase accuracy
6. Disruption-centered planning to predict performance during disruptions
7. Secure mobile communications
8. Integrated solutions for monitoring critical sensors of performance & thresholds
9. Dynamic scheduling to rapidly respond to changes in operations tempo
10. Sensitivity methods to chart "what if" scenarios and determine impact drivers
11. User-defined cost controls to administer limited resources and provide visibility into financial tracking at all levels of asset management
12. Consistent and transparent organization reporting structure for asset management, allowing for comparative analysis of asset treatment

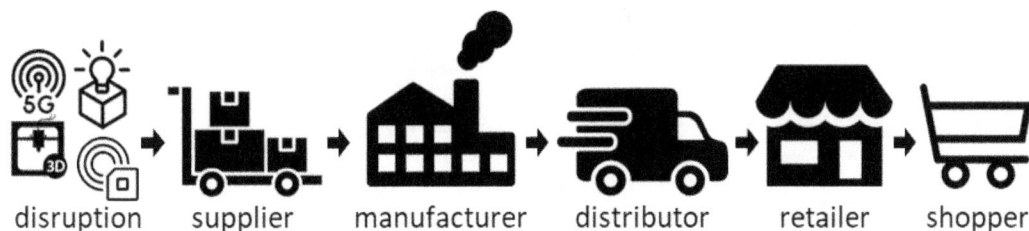

Figure 3: Simple Supply Chain Process

Solution. Let's begin by resolving the Supply Chain Manager's challenges using the technologies illustrated in Figure 4. A sample of the Supply Chain Manager's questions are:

1. What supply chain assets are mine?
2. What is my method of identification and/or ownership?
3. Where are my supply chain assets?
4. What are my supply chain assets doing?
5. What condition are my supply chain assets in?
6. What is my demand for service?
7. What environment are my assets in now and in the future?
8. Who and where are my supply chain users/customers?
9. Where are my supply chain facilities?
10. What resources are available to me and my supply chain?

Supply chain visibility (SCV) is at the forefront of business leaders' minds today. Businesses need to know where their product is, when it will be delivered, and every detail regarding the contents of their freight. It's also essential to provide this level of visibility to all the stakeholders in the supply chain. Plus, we want to automate the process to take advantage of the "no-touch" know-how. Hence, there is a need to introduce new technologies into the supply chain. Overwhelming?

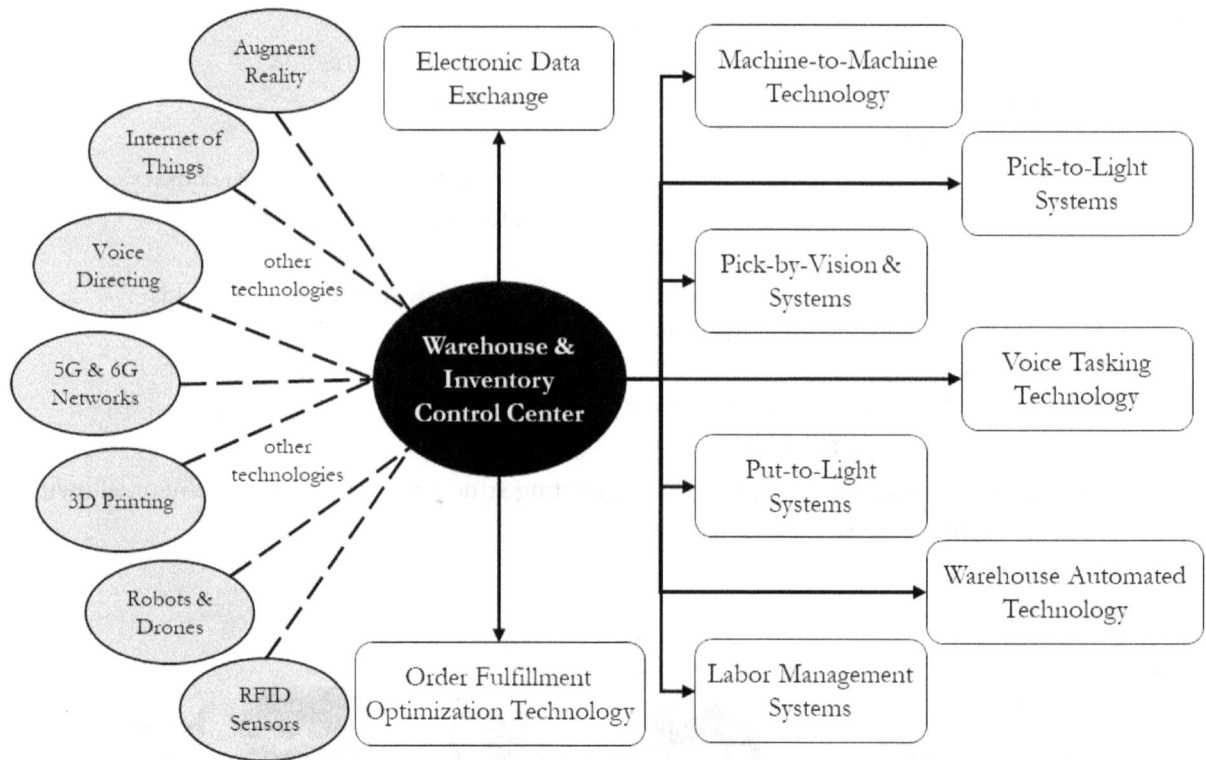

Figure 4: Supply Chain Technologies

Action. Where do I begin? With the end in mind! First, a reminder: before commencing any structured approach to transformation, agreement must be reached on the desired engagement outcome (s). The engagement outcome(s) must be clear, unequivocal, and measurable, with clearly defined success criteria and performance measures.

Summary. Whatever tools business leaders choose, companies operating in this environment cannot afford to be the last to respond to problems in their supply chain. Sustainability strategies throughout the supply chain demand attention.

The following chapters highlight key areas in which disruptions could occur. Those who prepare in advance can minimize the effects of an outside disruption while expediting the recovery. This could be the difference between advancing in the marketplace or shutting down for good. Are you prepared? Perhaps you will turn the outcome around and become the disruptor.

References & Bibliography. See below.

1. Southam, Mark, "Disruption as a Business Strategy - How to Harness the Power of Disruption," www.certifyassoc.com, May 2020

2. Joseph, David, "Challenges of Humanless Warehousing," Veridian.info, April 22, 2020 https://supplychaingamechanger.com/humanless-warehousing-tips-for-a-robot-driven-future/;

3. "A "Don't Touch" Strategy will Dramatically Lean out your Supply Chain!" Mortson Enterprises Inc. 4/22/20 https://supplychaingamechanger.com/global-process-excellence-part-5-adopt-no-touch-strategy-dramatically-lean-supply-chain/

4. Lofvers, Martijn, "Disruptive Advice," Supply Chain Movement, February 16, 2016; https://www.supplychainmovement.com/disruptive-advice/

5. "Top 10 Future Trends in Supply Chain and Logistics," October 31, 2019; https://www.aacb.com/trends-in-supply-chain-and-logistics/

6. O'Shaughnessy, Kim, "Future of Supply Chain Management: Experts Predict SCM Trends for 2020," February 26, 2019; https://www.selecthub.com/supply-chain-management/supply-chain-management-future-trends/

7. Lofvers, Martijn, "No-nonsense," Supply Chain Movement, November 18, 2018; https://www.supplychainmovement.com/no-touch-nonsense/

8. Swedberg, Claire, "RFID and Blockchain Bring Shared Visibility to Supply Chain," RFID Journal, March 2, 2020

9. "The Elegance of the Costco Supply Chain!", supplychaingamechanger.com, posted on March 28, 2020

10. "Warehouse Fulfillment – Move Material to the People, Not Vice Versa!", supplychaingamechanger.com, posted on March 16, 2020

11. "What's the Difference Between Fulfillment and Replenishment?," supplychaingamechanger.com, posted on February 19, 2020

12. Hasty, Jen, "What Is a SKU Number and How Retailers Can Use Them to Boost Their Business," Shopify, August 30, 2018; https://www.shopify.com/retail/what-is-a-sku-number

13. Stephanie Davies, "7 critical KPIs for the best supply chain management process," LinkedIn; January 7, 2015

Category: Technology

Truth #1. Technology changes will impact your operations.

Background & Introduction. Technology disruption is the influence of new digital technologies and business models on existing goods, services, systems, and structures. Of course, this shift is not happening overnight, but it's fair to say that the impact of digital technologies is increasing exponentially. Some of the characteristics are listed below.

- A disruptive technology supersedes an older process, product, or habit.
- It usually has superior attributes that are immediately obvious, at least to early adopters.
- Rather than established companies, upstarts are the usual source of disruptive technologies.
- Disruptive technology attracts a limited audience, has performance issues, and has unproven practical applications.

These events can be a disaster or a massive success for an organization. The devastating part of disruption is when a new technology destroys a business. The positive side of disruption is the process in which new technologies or new kinds of products overthrow previous products and create a new company. Figure 5 provides a few examples of disruption-capable technologies.

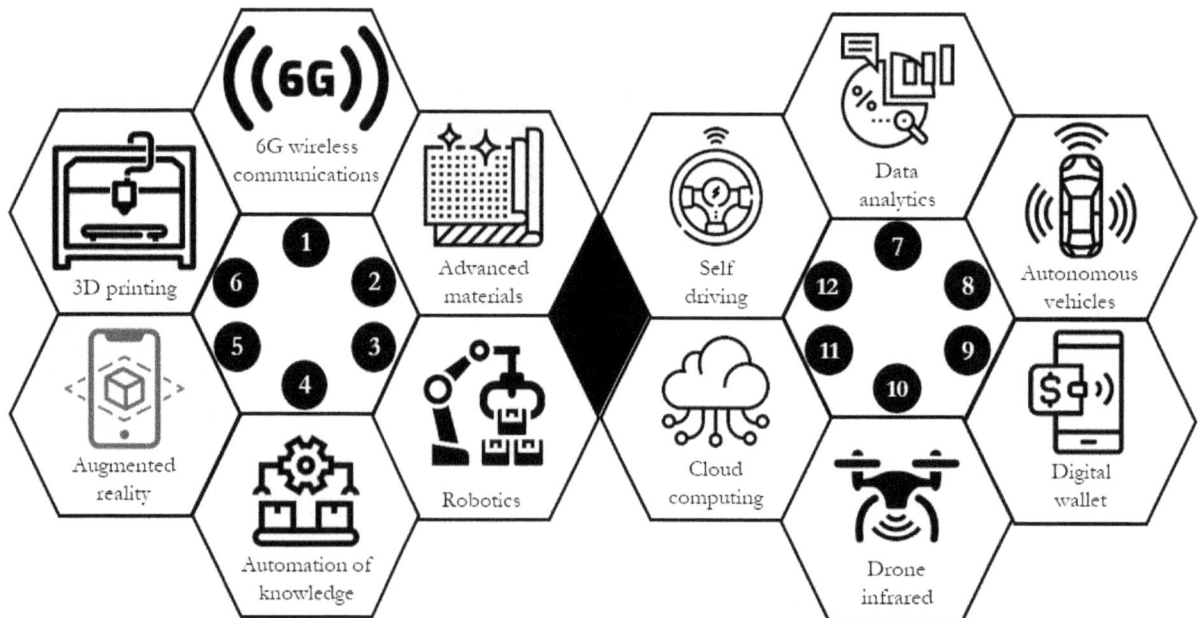

Figure 5: Examples of New Technologies that are Disrupting the Marketplace

Another way to say this is that technology disruption describes a method where a product or service initially takes root in simple applications at the bottom of a market, typically by being less expensive and more accessible and then relentlessly moving upmarket. It eventually displaces established competitors.

No one can know the future, but it is possible to derive outcomes based on past and current observations. Companies that prepare for disruption are the most likely to survive and even thrive post-disruption.

A large part of preparing for disruption is a change in mindset and/or new culture for the workplace. Imagine looking at your customers through the lens of the "Jobs to be Done" theory. 'Customers don't purchase products based solely on their attributes, but rather, "hire" products to do "jobs" they need to get done.' Another aspect is vigilance in the vast flow of products that comprise the Internet of Things (IoT), Operational Technology (OT), and the Industrial IoT. There are two ways that disruption appears in the marketplace.

1. **Low-End Disruption.** This occurs when a company uses a low-cost business model to enter the bottom of an existing market and claims a segment.
2. **New-Market Disruption.** Another type of disruptive innovation is new-market disruption when a company creates a new segment in an existing market with a low-cost product.

Both approaches significantly influence the future, whether successful or not.

Purpose. This chapter presents a couple of pathways for organizations to employ when preparing for technology disruptions that will influence their business operations.

Challenge. Detection, mitigation, recovery, and reconstruction largely depend on how well we are prepared to handle technology disruption. Unlike prevention, they involve measures that limit the disruption's effects and facilitate recovery. Preparing for disruption is straightforward. Be aware and know the industry, company, workforce, community, and regulations. Become a student of consumer purchasing options and conveniences. Technology disruption can impact the office (see Figure 6) and the factory (see Figure 7).

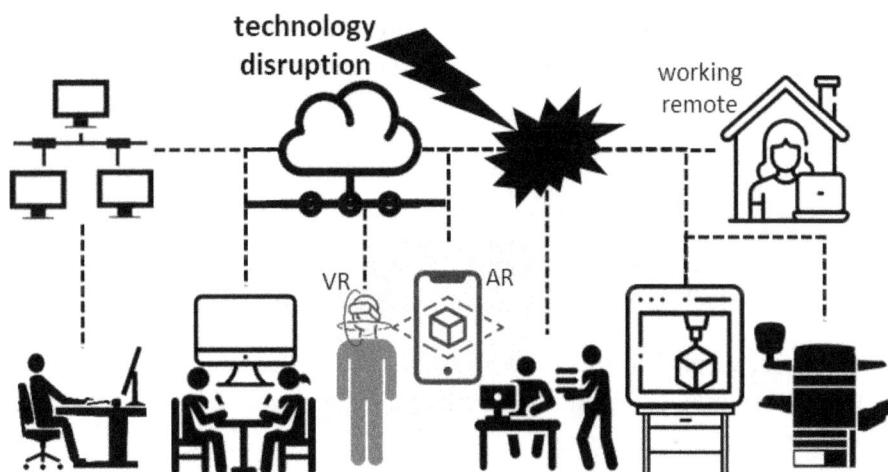

Figure 6: Technology Disruption in an Office Environment

Description. A technology disruption is intricately linked to the concept of risk. Disruption concerns the consequences of that risk: the risk that damage will occur and be disastrous. Disruptive technology becomes successful because of the following:

1. Business models are innovative. The business model targeting low-end customers or a new segment of customers will aid in the success of disruptive technology.
2. The highest priority is a value network. A network of suppliers, customers, and distributors prospers when it succeeds.
3. Enabling technologies fuel the disruption preparation engine. Disruptive technology should be able to make products accessible and affordable to a bigger audience.
4. 'Datafication' has changed everything, especially consumers' expectations and business culture. This includes selling, purchasing, and delivering products and services.

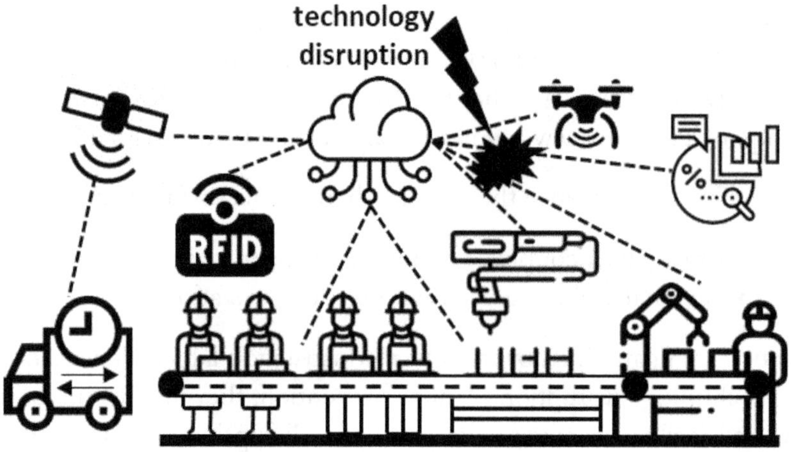

Figure 7: Technology Disruption Affects the Factory Workplace

The number of connections, products, services, and actors means that systems are becoming increasingly complex and challenging to understand and quickly bring under control. Physical and digital systems are inextricably linked; as operational and digital technologies merge, cyber security (securing systems) engage, and safety (the safety and reliability of systems) require faster response times; these have become intertwined.

Solution. The steps below provide a long-term planning framework for a technology disruption. See Figure 8.

Accept that disruption is inevitable. It might be tempting to hope the challenges of digital disruption will decrease, but all signs suggest disruption will be the new normal.

Watch other industries. Digital disruption has already taken place in many sectors. It involves an entrepreneurial brand marketing a product or service to a client whose behavior and expectations significantly differ from two decades ago.

Be curious about your industry. As with all technology, it will become more sophisticated and cheaper over time—study emerging technologies and models within your industry.

Learn how disruptors disrupt. There are no secrets regarding digital disruptors' tools to gain a foothold in markets. Learning about these tools can provide insight into a process that works for your business.

Explore new markets. Open the door to a market segment otherwise unavailable to your products and services.

Get close to your customers. Staying close to customers keeps them loyal, and you may see them advocating on your behalf. Happy customers can also act as a testbed for your ideas, enabling you to test concepts quickly and inexpensively.

Capture and use data. Companies that win in digital disruption are often best at gathering and using data to a competitive advantage. Capture customer data in such a way that generates new insights.

Find partners. The complexity of technology disruption means it is impossible to take on all possibilities on your own.

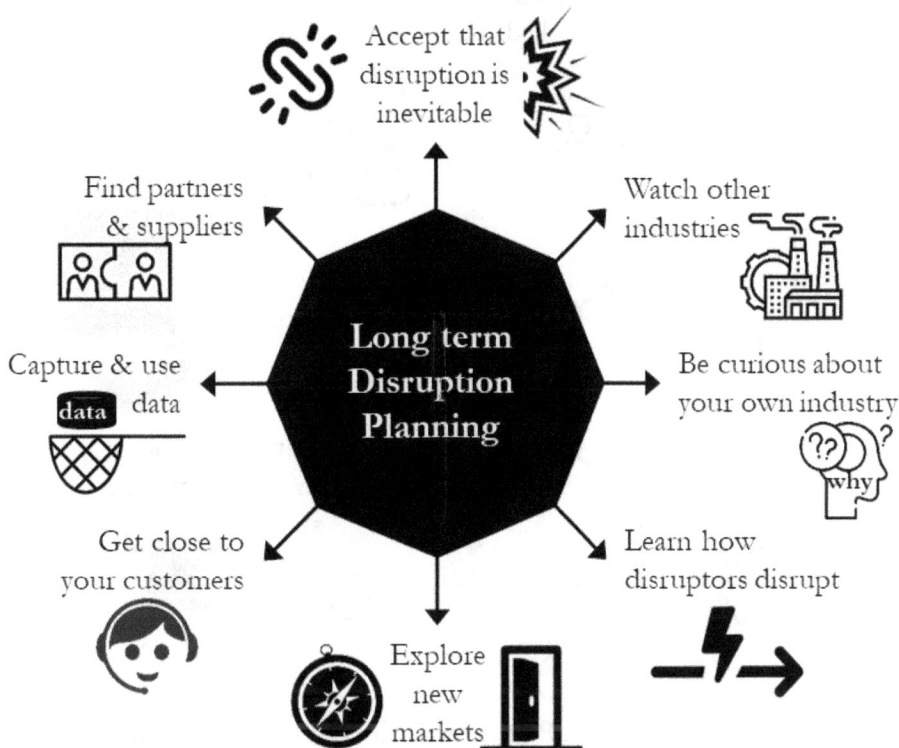

Figure 8: Long-Term Planning for Technology Disruption

Another approach to technology disruption is short-term planning. See Figure 9.

Identify fallback options. Are your immediate backup equipment and processes in order? Is your data backed up on off-campus storage? Have you tested your backup power arrangements, and are you constantly protecting your multiple sources and options, such as with suppliers? Are you conducting cross-skill training to give your workforce more tools to handle disruption?

Re-examine your technology isolation for protection. Are your network firewalls secure, are employees protecting their access to the technologies, and are risks minimized during employee turnovers? Does your organization practice cyber hygiene?

Communicating with all stakeholders and keeping them informed is the best way to determine what is happening and how to respond.

Detect disruption using early-warning systems. The early detection of disruptive events is important because the longer the signs go unnoticed, the greater the potential for damage. Remember to share information between leadership and the workforce.

Scrutinize lessons learned. Technology risks are relatively new and remain difficult to identify and evaluate. Nevertheless, necessary steps have been taken in recent years to share information on innovative devices, software applications, digital security measures, vulnerabilities, and disruptive incidents.

Record and document actions and activities. Encourage all actors to note their actions, concerns, and outcomes and archive them when convenient. Distribute this information to better understand what happened, why, what worked, and what didn't work.

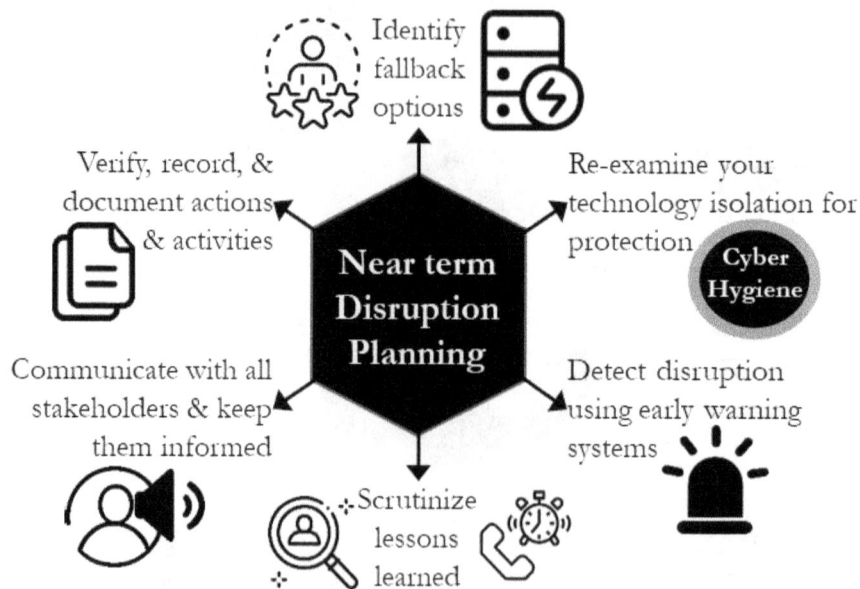

Figure 9: Short-Term Planning for Technology Disruption

Summary. Technology has taken center stage in the success and failure of companies today. New businesses have changed how we live, shop, work and consume content. Innovation is happening faster than ever before. With economic uncertainty, it's become even more crucial for businesses to deploy innovative technology to maintain competitiveness. Be prepared.

References & Bibliography.

1. Monica Charlton, "Digital Disruption and Why You Need to be Upskilling Now," Polyglot Group; June 17, 2020
2. Amy Rosen and Matt Ezold, "Workplace Interrupted People, Technology, and Change," Work Design Magazine; June 20, 2020
3. Marcell Vollmer, "Disruption, the changing workplace and the future of automation," IT Pro Portal; December 12, 2019
4. Tim Smith, "Disruptive Technology Definition," Investopedia; April 2, 2022
5. Daniel Burrus, "Digital Disruption and Your Workforce," Burrus Research; March 21, 2018
6. Catherine Cote, "What Is Disruptive Innovation," HBS Online; September 3, 2020
7. "Disruptive Technology - Overview, Examples, Success Factors," CFI; January 14, 2022
8. Erik Schrijvers, "Preparing for Digital Disruption," Springer; 2021
9. "The top 8 ways to prepare for digital disruption," Macquarie; 2021

Category: Technology

Truth #2. You will experience malicious cyber activity.

Background & Introduction. Global economies are experiencing unprecedented technological change, including an explosion in automation, the takeoff of artificial intelligence, and rapid advances in fields such as cybersecurity. This disruption affects almost every aspect of society—from industrial strategies and competitiveness to the labor market and how your organization functions.

Malicious cyber activity touches your business operations in all phases daily. Every company should be prepared for the inevitable cybersecurity breach or incident. These can be a data breach, data ransom, system failure, and corporate espionage. Many businesses value the importance of a crisis management plan for cybersecurity disruption. The impact is felt across several business operations at once. A malicious disruption hits an organization and creates both near-term and long-term problems. We aren't discussing a software flaw, a system power surge, or forgotten passwords. A malicious cyber disruption potentially creates a disaster. Your company will struggle to walk away unscathed. These activities seek to compromise or impair the confidentiality, integrity, or availability of computers, information or communications systems, networks, physical or virtual infrastructure controlled by computers or information systems, or information resident thereon. Malware, denial of service, and banking Trojans are examples. Recently, this seems to occur more often and with a more significant impact.

Modern-day industrial operations often span complex IT (information technology) and OT (operational technology) infrastructures. In a standard environment, thousands of devices are increasingly connected via the Industrial Internet of Things (IIoT). This creates new challenges in securing industrial environments, making cybersecurity threats even more difficult to detect, investigate, and remediate. Many industrial organizations have begun to converge their IT and OT groups. See Figure 10. The IT/OT convergence trend is not only driving the integration of IT tools with OT solutions but also requires alignment of the strategic goals, collaboration, and training; this is only the beginning of the challenge.

The best strategy is to be prepared for malicious cyber activities from bad actors. Reduce your attack surface.

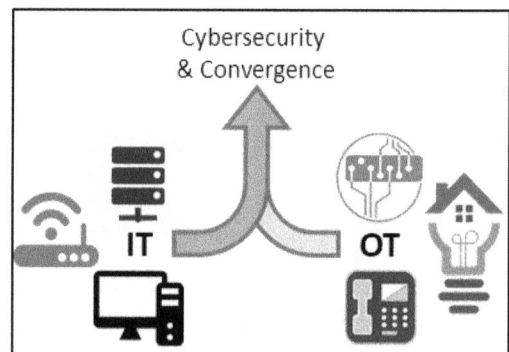

Figure 10: IT versus OT

16

Purpose. This chapter examines approaches for organizations to reach a reasonable and affordable readiness posture to elevate their preparedness for disruption caused by malicious cyber activities. The strategy centers around the CERTIFY methodology, which describes a proven framework of steps to achieve this goal. Furthermore, this paper discusses this structure in context with a cyber-attack – resulting in disruption. The main objective is to provide the leader with a depiction of being prepared for disruption.

Challenge. An integrated threat management strategy reflects an in-depth understanding of the cascading impacts of interconnected cyber-physical infrastructure. As technology evolves rapidly, it increasingly links physical and cyber assets. Both IT and OT are vulnerable to malicious cyber activity. This increases the attack surface and the number of all possible points or attack vectors where an unauthorized user can access a system and cause damage. Convergence reduces the number of total vulnerabilities and consolidates the organization's IT and OT staff to achieve the same goal – cyber protection. Preparation is the best defense against disruption caused by malicious cyber activities. This is our challenge.

IT and OT environments must now collaborate to address security threats on both sides of the network. Furthermore, they must collaborate to stop the lateral creep of an attack that may have started in one environment and successfully spread to the other. Table 1 provides some examples of aspects of each technology.

Solution. Adapting to change can be a big challenge for many businesses. However, as disruptive transformations turn many industries upside down, adaptability is increasingly essential for entrepreneurs. Change is the only constant in the business world, so preparation is necessary.

We don't overcome disruption by being more vital or intelligent than our competitors but by being better able to adapt to it. The steps below are things an organization can do to prepare for disruption caused by malicious cyber activities. The first step is creating a disruption plan to prevent and mitigate cyber-attacks. See the checklist below and use CERTIFY, as shown in Figure 11, for a straightforward approach to an organization's disruption plan.

1. Get prepared ahead of time by producing a cyber disruption plan.
2. Assign cyber disruption roles to your team.
3. Run cyber-attack scenarios through a series of storyboard-like exercises.
4. Maintain cyber hygiene, inspect safety features, and safeguard emergency supplies.
5. Install cybersecurity software.
6. Establish a strict password policy.
7. Learn and apply the National Institute of Standards and Technology's cybersecurity framework. See part of Figure 11.
8. Ensure minimal administrative privileges.
9. Train employees, including the leadership structure.
10. Document plans, record actions, conduct an exercise, & discuss lessons learned.

Description. Businesses must navigate the financial and operational challenges of disruption while rapidly addressing the needs of their people, customers, and suppliers. Organizational leaders can turn massive complexity and business disturbance into meaningful change by taking the right actions. See Figure 11 for creating an action and recovery plan.

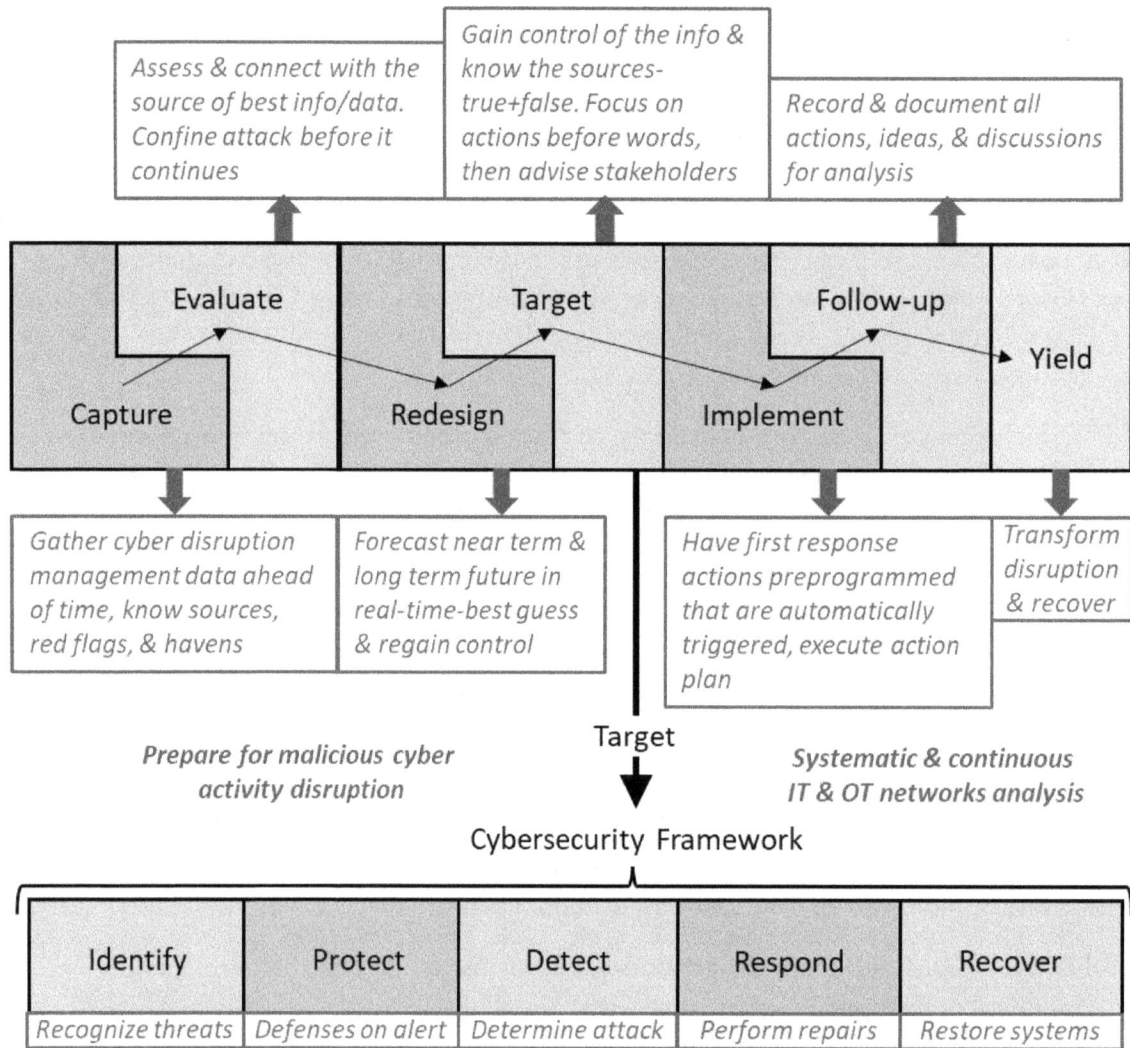

Figure 11: Cyber Disruption Action Plan Utilizing CERTIFY

Actions. A business can take many directions when trying to improve disruption readiness. It is important to remember that these are unpredictable situations. See Table 1 for a brief list of cybersecurity actions an organization can accomplish.

Table 1: Cybersecurity Actions

Communication	Coordination	Collaboration
Initiate a dialogue with management	Formalize roles & responsibilities	Devote resources (time & funding) to complete
Assign leadership roles for convergence efforts	Identify linked assets & assess risk levels	Prioritize improvements & seek automation chances
Establish team e.g. CSO, CISO, IT, & security	Conduct vulnerability assessment	Develop risk driven policies & best practices

Summary. A malicious cyber activity disruption (by definition) will be a surprise. But your plan of attack should already be prepared. Your organization will be judged on how it responds. You'll need a disruption plan and a disruption response team. You'll need trained personnel and social media monitoring. You'll need damage limitation to protect the reputation of your company.

References and Bibliography.

1. "7 Types of Cyber Security Threats," University of North Dakota; 2020
2. Jefferson, Brian, "The 15 Most Common Types of Cyber Attacks," Lepide; 8/6/2021
3. "Cybersecurity and Physical Security Convergence," Cybersecurity & Infrastructure Security Agency (CISA); 2019
4. APRIL 7, 2020
5. "IT OT Convergence – Benefits and Challenges in Manufacturing," INSIGHTS IOT; 2020
6. Yusuph Kileo, "2021 Cybersecurity Checklist: Protect Your Systems and Networks from a Cyberattack," in January 6, 2021

Category: Technology

Truth #3. Communication channels will change.

Background & Introduction. Communication, as we know, is being disrupted. It lives at the center of our universe and has driven our lives, both business-to-business (B2B) and business-to-consumer (B2C), to a simple everyday existence, sometimes referred to as peer-to-peer (P2P). Social, mobile, big data, and the cloud have changed our lives and how we communicate and will continue to revolutionize the future of business enterprise. See Figure 12.

Disruptive communication may have a negative connotation, but it provides a net positive for most people in the business world and everyday life. However, ensuring success in disruptive communication requires that companies listen to customers and ensure employees are on board to achieve company goals.

Moving into the future, communication disruption will continue. Not just how we communicate with those we know, but also those we don't know. The way companies will market to individuals and how we as individuals gain access to our digital assets. Our lives are amidst a storm of disruption, but to some extent, it has become so ubiquitous in our existence that we may not even realize it. Case in point are the commonly used conference tools such as Zoom, teams, and Facetime.

Figure 12: Communication Disruption Impacts Many Channels

Both internal and external communications are being disrupted in the business world. Within the past few years, companies have seen a heavy dependence on tools such as Slack and HipChat, both of which are intended for inter-team communications.

Another disruption in the business marketplace is business-to-customer communication. The other business-to-customer communication disruption resides on the business's website: in-app messengers, such as live chat.

While plenty of business communications are "business as usual," it's clear that the space is rapidly changing. Business communication is shifting away from its dependence on old-school email technology and traditional communication methods, as companies are quickly becoming more receptive to newer communication methods in real-time across various unique and promising platforms.

Purpose. Influential communication leaders are the key to adapting and disrupting your business to take advantage of disruption in the marketplace. An organization can create products and services that delight customers and improve its brand through effective communication and co-innovation. This chapter aims to discuss the effect of communication change on your business. In addition, it provides some tips on how to be prepared and respond to the negative aspects of disruption.

Challenges. Disruption changes business models and the way people think and act. It requires people to adapt to the new ways of communication. Disruption leads to the emergence of new ideas and expectations and requires companies to be creative and innovate. It also requires businesses to keep up-to-date and stay ahead of current trends, thereby being competitive and desirable for their customers. Disruption happens because of technology, gadgets, automation of processes, social media, or innovations in terms of products and services. The other side of communication channel disruption is when these new and innovative means to communicate fail, staying in business while the problem is mitigated and lessened. This is the challenge organizations face today and tomorrow.

Solution. The rise of technologies has changed the communication industry, and we're also talking about digital communication. Digitalization is a significant part of people's lives—from smartphones, tablets, personal computers, and gadgets to home assistants, voice recognition systems, personal finance, health tools, and many more. It's no surprise that the communication channels have been changing. See Figure 13.

Businesses now talk to customers using emojis, gifs, stickers, and hashtags. They employ new channels such as social media, mobile apps, native advertising, and all types of videos (YouTube, pop-up ads, etc.). Finally, how content is generated and distributed includes big data analysis of consumer behavior and interests, plus content marketing automation. Now add 5G, Operation Technology (OT) devices, smartphone innovations, encryption, cyber hygiene, and voila – an armful of potential disruption.

The solution is multi-faceted, requires sophisticated expertise, and demands constant attention from the business leader(s). First and foremost, you need a plan, that is, a dynamic disruption communication plan. Next, a unique team of experts is dedicated to communicating with consumers, media, bloggers, influencers,

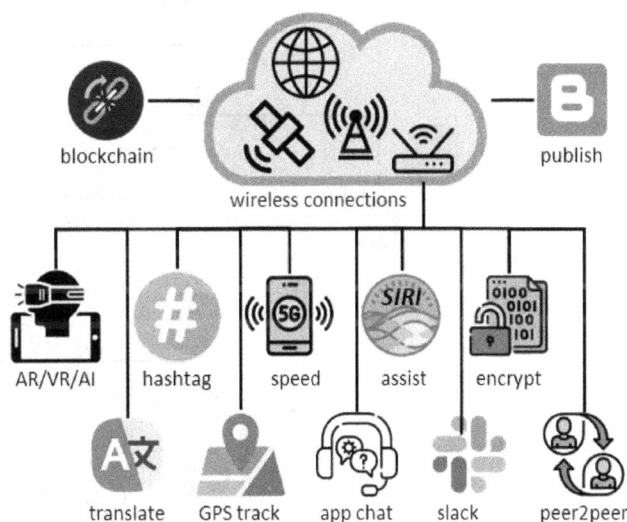

Figure 13: Many of the New Means of Communications Today

stakeholders, employees, communities, and regulators. Constantly test for trends for industry innovations, and remember new products arrive every day.

Get ahead of disruption. Then, turn it in your favor and create an opportunity.

Description. With in-app messengers, customers can start a one-on-one conversation with a company by clicking on the message bubble at the bottom right-hand side of the page. They can either converse with the brand or read a message the brand has pushed to the customer.

Behind the scenes, though, is where the magic happens: in-app messengers can determine customer data, such as where the user has logged in from, social media account information, pages the customer has visited, and the number of times the customer has visited the site, among other exciting statistics, to inform companies better how to respond to the customer. This also helps with a push messaging strategy, allowing companies to target specific messaging to individuals based on location and behavior.

Actions. The communications industry is in the throes of a disruption. Over-the-top (OTT) digital giants and new startups have upset the status quo. The transition to Industry 4.0 offers new communication options and alternative access technologies. The digital transformation to blend, integrate, and connect with myriad new technological advances can be mind-boggling. However, there are steps that organizations can take to prepare for this eventuality. A few of these are listed below. See Figure 14.

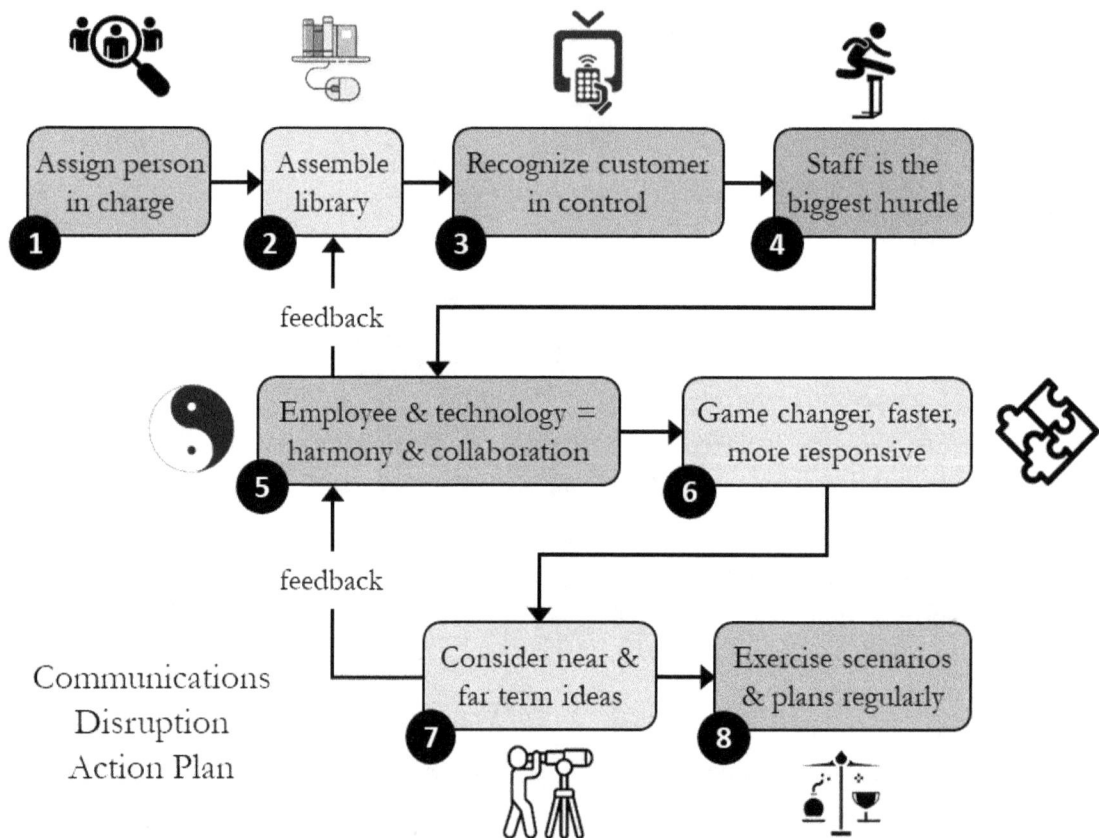

Figure 14: Steps to Consider for Communication Channel Disruption Plan

1. Assign a Communications Channel Awareness officer. This becomes an additional duty for the chief of information, director of technology, and/or chief of new products within a company.
2. Assemble a digital library of data, information, lessons learned, articles, specialized knowledge, and accumulated wisdom on past, present, and forecasted communication innovations.
3. Recognize that each advancement continues to place the customer more in charge of means, methods, and delivery of communications.
4. As with all workplace changes, realize that the employees, stakeholders, and executive staff are the first and most challenging hurdles to surviving a transformative disruption. Thus, transparency, honesty, and openness create a much better climate for success.
5. Acknowledge that industry convergence (IT and OT), cyber security vulnerability, and the pace of technology innovation are game-changing forces. They impact and fragment value chains and create faster, more responsive supply chains.
6. Remember that a communications ecosystem is an interconnected and interdependent network of diverse entities that spurs innovation in sustaining the technology environment. This step emphasizes that integrating technologies must be in harmony with companywide collaboration.
7. Exercise possible scenarios, internal action plans, and each mix of business structures to improve response times and reduce communication mishaps. Practice these regularly, record the results, and take photos.
8. Extend your plan beyond the near term. Visualize a multi-pronged approach by examining the now, the next, and the possible.

Summary. Ultimately, computing is about networked intelligence, and the real impact of the Internet, IIoT, and OT devices will occur once that translates into automation and machine intelligence. So, cognitive computing will transform our world. It is time to prepare and stay prepared for disruption in our communications channels.

References & Bibliography.

1. Daniel Newman, "4 Technology Trends Disrupting How We Communicate," Forbes CMO; May 13, 2014
2. "Disruptive Communication in Today's Digital World," USC Online MCM; 2022
3. "Flexible Pathways for Today's Communication Leaders," USC Annenberg University School of Communication - brochure; 2022
4. Jerry Goldman, "How Messaging Is Disrupting Business Communication," Inc.com; February 2, 2016
5. Iva Grigova, "Disruptive PR: The New Way of Doing Public Relations," Prowley; 2022
6. "Outthinking disruption in communications; The 2020 CSP in the cognitive era," IBM Institute for Business Value; 2021

Category: Competition
Truth #4. A competitor will develop a better business model.

Background & Introduction. What is a disruptive business model? Disruptive business models are disruptive innovations that bring a new idea or technology to an existing market. Disruptive market entrants usually capture unmet demands in the existing market.

Disruptive innovation powers business models, helping them create a new niche within an existing market or a new market altogether by creating, disintermediating, refining, reengineering, or optimizing a product/service.

A business model is a plan for how a company will make money. It can be simple or very complicated. The components of a business model include details on all operations and short—and long-term visions for the business' growth. With a business model, investors and owners will have a clear idea of how to grow the industry best, and it will be much easier to create a stable and sustainable concern.

The wild card that is looming is business model disruption. The business model needs to engage both ways; see Figure 15. It must survive a challenge from a competitor and thrive by innovating a disruption of its own. That is a tough challenge, but it can be done. Some noticeable examples are Target, Apple, United Airlines, and Netflix.

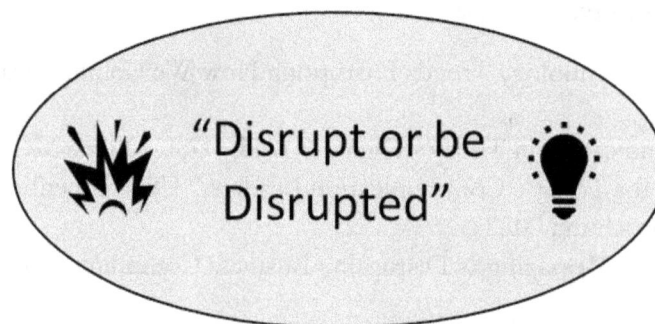

Figure 15: Silicon Valley Quote of the 21st Century

Purpose. Disruptive business models by one or more competitors can force you out of business or bankrupt you (see Figure 16). It is necessary to stay informed about your products and services, customers, surroundings, and geopolitical environment. This chapter discusses business model disruption and provides suggestions to consider when creating your business model, redesigning your model, or facing a competitor assailing your market share.

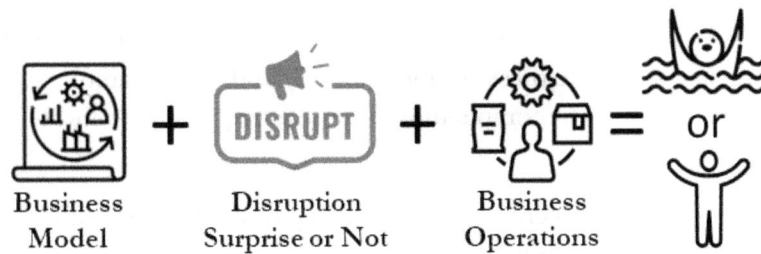

Figure 16: Business Model Must Adapt to Disruption

Challenges. There are two situations. The company has a business model; thus, the challenge is to conduct a transformation, or the company needs a business model, and a formulation is required. The two means are different, but the business model elements are straightforward. Further complicating this issue is that the business model needs to survive, attack a competitor, and be adaptable to seize the innovation and capture a new market. The confrontation involves several elements with the organization and buy-in from each group. First, let's describe the business model.

Description. The business model has several elements, and different situations, environments, and industries require something similar. The research for this chapter reveals anywhere from 3-12 elements in a good business model. Table 2 lists some of these elements to help you understand your company's requirements.

8 Elements	5 Elements #1	7 Elements
Value Proposition	Identify Target Market	Establish business processes
Revenue Model	Identify Value Chain	Record key business resources
Market Opportunity	Mobilize Resources	Develop a strong value proposition
Competitive Environment	Identify Business Partners	Develop a strong value proposition
Competitive Advantage	Keep Business Model Flexible	Determine key business partners
Market Strategy		Create a demand generation strategy
Organization Development	5 Elements #2	Leave room for innovation
Management Team	Value Proposition & Market	
	Value Chain Structure	4 Elements
3 Elements	Revenue Generation Strategies	Target Audiences
Deliver results	Position in the Market	Market Offering
Company Time	Long-Term Strategy	Organization Essence
Customer Money		Unique Strategic Position

Table 2: Examples of Business Model Elements

Successful disruptive business models often focus on the customer again. New technologies have changed customer behavior, and thus, this change also enables models to meet these needs. Many successful companies also combine these business models and use different models for different parts of their companies. The right combination of innovative products and business models can play a significant role in success.

There are many business models to choose from; see Figure 17. This list of disruptive business models is neither exhaustive nor complete. The figure shows nine important business models for essential innovations in many markets. The goal is to understand business models and fundamental principles. See Figure 18 for the basic principles.

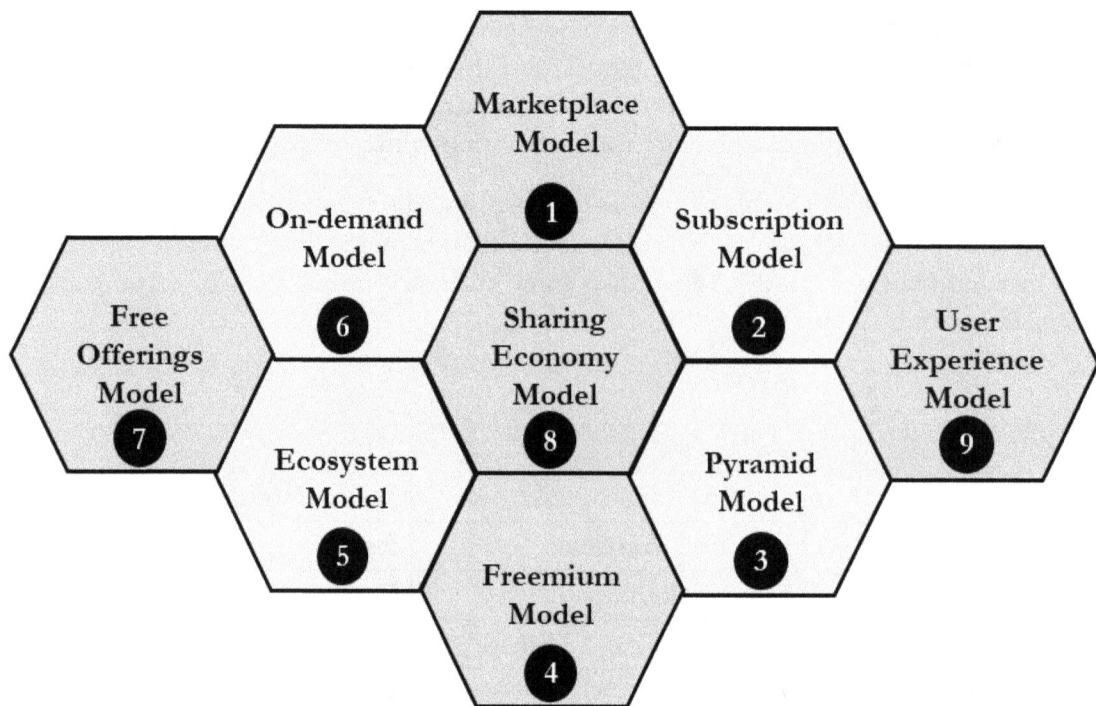

Figure 17: Nine Different Types of Business Models

Disruptive business models are innovations that bring a new idea or technology to an existing market. Disruptive market entrants usually capture unmet demand in the existing market.

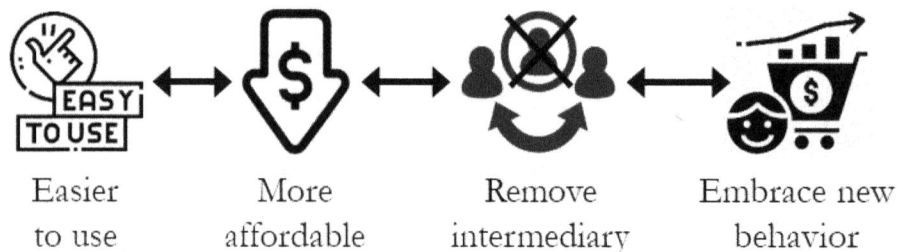

Figure 18: Disruptive Business Model Basic Principles

Solution. Prepare a disruption plan that focuses on the business model. The disruption may discuss some of the considerations in the list below. Remember, it is a dynamic plan that changes all the time. The source for change may be the organization, the labor force, government regulations, the environment, and/or the supply chain. See Figure 19.

1. Research disruption as it relates to the business model selected.
2. Determine what customers are seeking. Most customers don't know what they want.
3. Learn what current market players are ignoring.
4. Ascertain whether customers will accept your solution or not.
5. Formulate a strategy - a foolproof plan to outperform competitors.
6. Obtain buy-in from the stakeholders and state the goals and expected outcomes.
7. Husband the available resources.
8. Execute the marketing plan utilizing the business model.
9. Create disruption!

Below are a few definitions relative to Figure 19. Figure 19 is a graphic that suggests an ideal value proposition and the environment to which it must adapt.

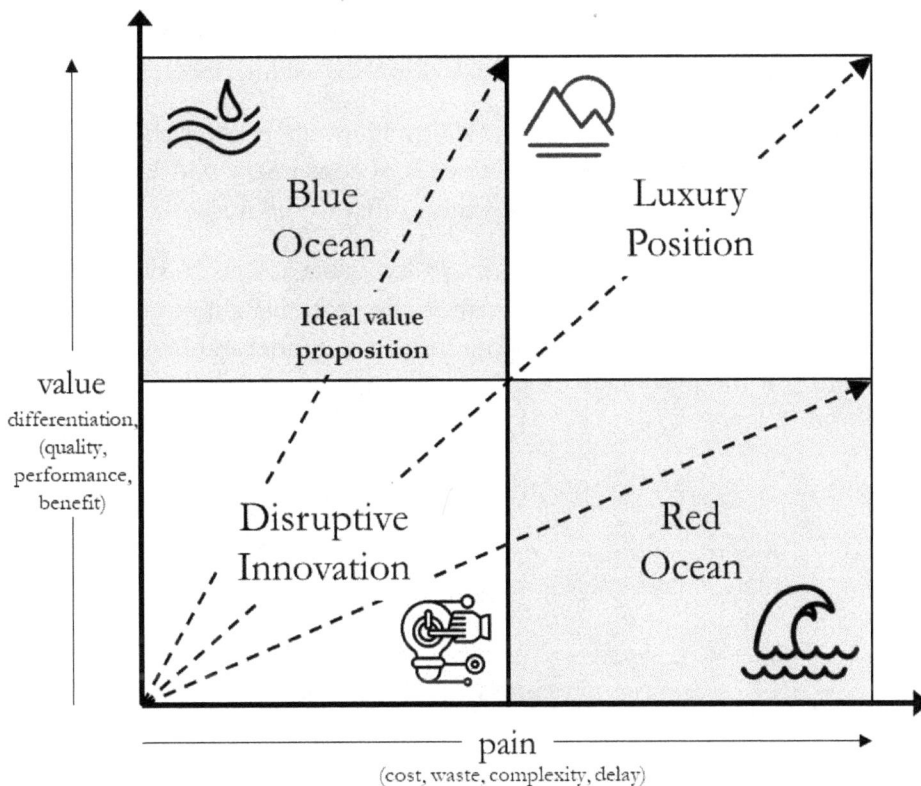

Figure 19: Disruptive Business Model Comparing Pain versus Value

Disruptive innovation is when a new product or service performs better at a lower cost than existing offerings, transforming the industry.

A **value proposition** explains how a product fills a need, communicates the added benefits, and states why it's better. The ideal value proposition appeals to a customer's strongest decision-making drivers.

Pain points are problems faced by current or prospective customers in the marketplace. They include any issues the company or customer may experience until a product or service is delivered.

Product **differentiation** is a tactic that helps businesses develop a competitive advantage and define compelling, unique selling propositions (USPs) that set their products apart from competitors' products.

Blue Ocean describes a new market with little competition or barriers standing in the way of innovators. An innovation appears in a vast "empty ocean" of market options and opportunities.

Red oceans are where industry boundaries are defined, and companies try to outperform their rivals. Cutthroat competition turns the ocean bloody red.

Luxury position is a segment in the retail industry that specializes in selling high-end goods characterized by high quality, high prices, and a high degree of exclusivity.

Summary. The best disruptive business model ideas come from the knowledge of repressed market demands. Repressed market demands refer to the needs of consumers who are already using a product but are not fully satisfied with it or lack features that would make the consumer's life easier.

Only an innovation that can make people's lives more accessible at a justified cost can form the base of the disruptive business model. Creating a new market by offering a new utility isn't easy. However, once the pain point is found, developing a business model and becoming a pioneer brings in a lot of public attention and plays a vital role in marketing.

References & Bibliography.

1. Benjamin Talin, "9 disruptive business models explained – new opportunities for companies: Consider changing the business model with changing economies around you," MoreThanDigital; April 7, 2022
2. Denis Oakley, "How to Survive Business Model Disruption," Denis Oakley & Co; April 15, 2019
3. Rahul Bhadana, "What Is Disruptive Business Model?" Feedough; November 3, 2020
4. Marc de Jong and Menno van Dijk, "Disrupting beliefs: A new approach to business-model innovation," McKinsey; July 1, 2015
5. Denis Oakley, "5 Step Business Model Innovation: Design a Radically Different Company v1.0," Denis Oakley & Co. v1.0; 2021
6. Loraine Couturier, "8 Key Elements Of A Business Model that You Should Understand," StartUp Mindset; February 22, 2022
7. Larry Alton, "The 7 Elements of a Strong Business Model." Entrepreneur; April 22, 2015
8. "Components of a Business Model," Chron; July 19, 2021
9. Xavier Camps "The Challenges of Transforming the Business Model," Glocalthinking; October 18, 2018

Category: Competition

Truth #5. A competitor will develop a better product.

Background & Introduction. If you're a business leader, you know it's hard to stand out from the crowd today! Technology, the internet, and constant access to mobile devices have made it challenging to get noticed by consumers who are inundated with brand advertising and content, not to mention the average attention span of today's shoppers.

Disruptive innovation transforms and even replaces industry-standard products with a new product. New or smaller brands often need to get ahead by interrupting the market and developing a better product. Knowledge derived from information about your market, employees, and community is at the heart of succeeding at such an endeavor. This is only done with data capture; make this a continuous process within your organization. See Figure 20.

A data-driven approach focuses decisions on facts rather than a hunch. It also offers measurable advantages and disadvantages. A data-driven approach relies on statistics and realities rather than intuition. Disruption is a theory of competitive response. It explains why some innovations cause competitors to attack while others stay off the radar until it's too late to compete. Disruption today can displace market leaders, their products, and their services. Responding to disruption means businesses need to think fast and react fast.

If your company's goal is to grow profitably, then you need to understand how to begin disrupting the markets it serves and, in the process, take market share away from competitors. Disruptive innovations are rarely Big Bang-type changes. Usually, there are more minor and incremental changes to existing products that customers perceive as offering better value than currently available. A big bang changeover is when a new system is embraced instantly, with no transition period

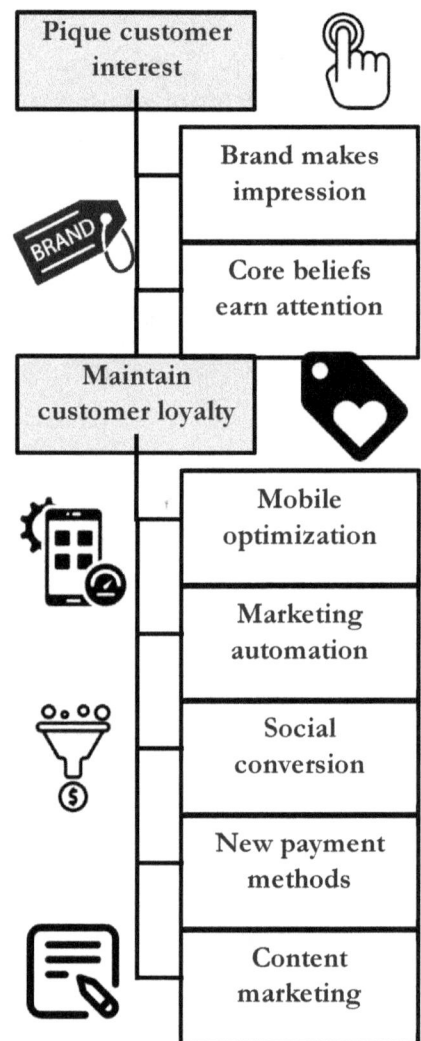

Figure 20: Data Topics to Capture Critical Knowledge for Competing

between the old and new systems. Big bang implementations have more risk than phased implementations because returning to the old system is more strenuous should anything go wrong.

Purpose. This chapter provides a framework for company decision-makers to improve their organization's readiness for disruption. No matter the number of innovations happening in today's marketplace, the key to riding the disruption wave in your industry is clearly understanding your market, competitors, and customers. We aim to offer an authoritative guide that discusses new product disruptions and a proposed solution for handling them. It guides businesses into focusing on what matters during disruption. This structured approach prevents competitors from disturbing your business with a new product.

Challenge. The best way to predict your organization's future is to create it. Companies must find ways to differentiate themselves from their competition. Businesses must think and act innovatively in a world where every product and service has competitors. Customers are looking for things that set companies apart, a discriminator. Some considerations to watch out for that may complicate the challenge are:

Figure 21: Analyze Data from All Sources

- Disruption and commoditization are closely associated. To commodify is to render (a good or service) widely available and interchangeable with one provided by another company.
- Disruptive innovation requires a separate strategic viewpoint.
- It isn't easy to achieve profitability quickly.
- Involves a detailed understanding of customer buying behavior.

This is the challenge business leaders face today. See Figure 21.

Description. The strength of a business success ecosystem is that you can only find success by fulfilling customer needs. Disruptive innovation often looks at future customers' needs before they realize they need them! Your competitor will disrupt your market if your business doesn't implement this approach. Gain knowledge from your activities. See Figure 22.

The collection and analysis of data form the basis of a data-driven strategy. It is easy to fall victim to assumptions or hidden biases while analyzing data. It is essential first to consider important metrics with which to measure progress. If you can't measure it - you can't improve it.

Here are some questions you can ask yourself to evaluate the disruptive potential of your product or your competitor's products and services.

- Are you and/or your existing competitors serving a significant, untapped need for the industry?
- Does your business model allow you to serve customers radically cheaper than existing competition?
- Will your future competitors write you off as low-quality, or do you consider your challenger to be offering low-quality products and services?
- As your product develops, will the quality increase to satisfy higher-value customers?

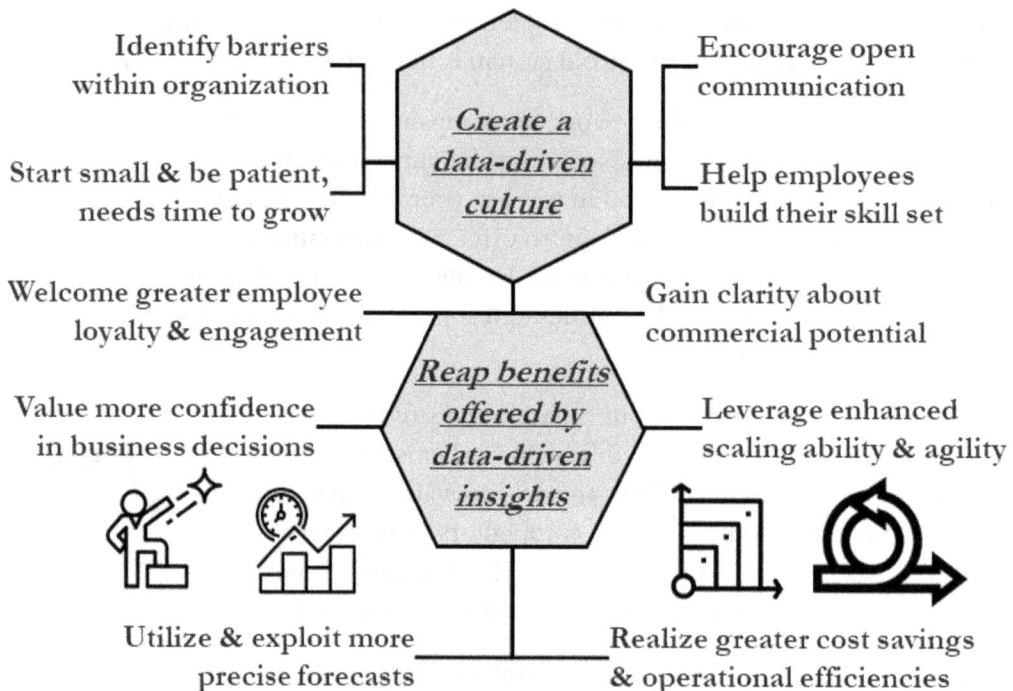

Figure 22: Suggested Actions for Framing the Disruption Plan

The response to the above questions may mean that you're resting on a potentially disruptive product or facing a rival with a disruptive product. To stave off contenders, don't compete on their definition of quality. Instead, focus on creating a business model that meets the demands of the underserved with higher quality.

Solution. The Framework, shown in Figure 23, guides chief decision-makers by focusing on what matters when responding to disruption. Doing so prevents a competitor from interrupting your market and damaging your business.

Five Steps to Predicting and Managing Disruptive Innovation

1. Examine closely the markets your company serves, the products sold, and the active competitors.
2. Realize that each product or service is a function of performance versus time.
3. Investigate customer buying behavior in your industry. Discover what changes are evident in the performance of products and services demanded by customers.
4. Find opportunities for disruption when the product performance offered by your competitors exceeds the performance demanded by customers; in other words, the performance versus time curve is different.
5. Develop products or services that meet the performance demanded by customers at a lower price and offer a better-perceived value.

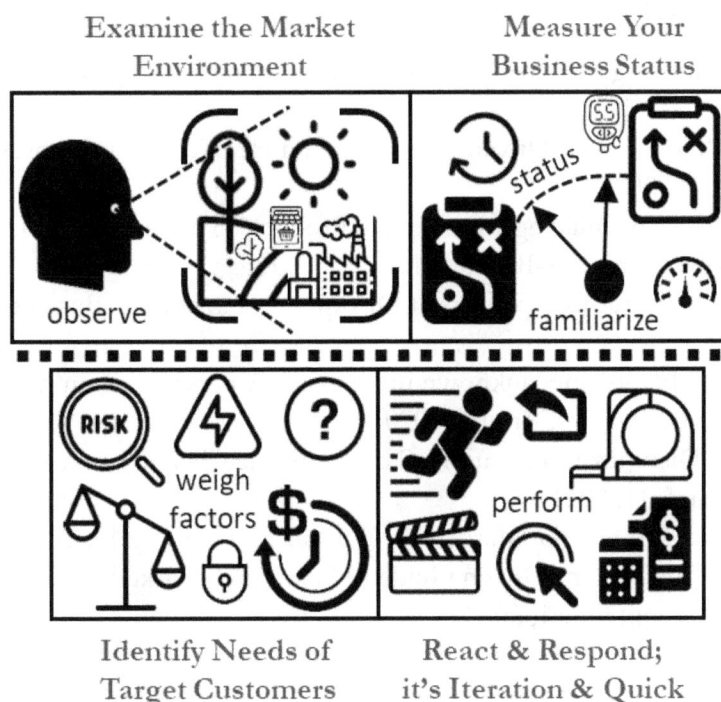

Figure 23: Suggested Solution for Continuous Monitoring of the Disruption Landscape

Summary. A data-driven business culture involves considering all critical work efforts to be motivated by the reality of data. The entire organization gains when each employee uses data to inform their decisions. You can reap the benefits of data-driven decisions and stay ahead of the curve by being ready for new products in your industry.

Although stopping disruption can be challenging, preparing for it will lessen the severity of a disruptive innovation. Having the right strategy can only take you so far; the company should also develop the right culture that embraces change and promotes innovation. Task your disruption team to monitor the changing market and your competitive advantage closely. This will ensure your business is prepared for disruption from your competitor developing a new product.

References & Bibliography.

1. Avery Phillips, "Marketing Strategies to Disrupt the Competition," The Next Scoop; April 16, 2018
2. Madhu Kesavan, "How a Data-Driven Approach Can Help Your Enterprises - A Detailed Guide," TNS; July 15, 2020
3. Dave Bailey, "The Key to Building a Disruptive Product," The Founder Coach; May 9, 2017
4. Ben Obear, "Top-10-Disruptive-Business-Models," Strategy; March 10, 2017
5. Ashton Bishop, "Beat Your Competitors at Disruptive Innovation," Business Strategy; October 5, 2019
6. Thibault Ducarme, "Identifying 'unknown unknowns': A perspective on non-traditional competition," Deloitte Insights; April 1, 2020
7. Robbie Richards, "Disruptive Innovation_ The Inevitable Change Every Market Must Face," MassChallenge; March 11, 2021
8. Charlie Alter, "5 Steps to Disrupt Markets," All business; February 17, 2022
9. Michael Brenner "The Content-Driven Guide to Disruptive Marketing [With Examples]," Marketing Insider Group; June 1, 2022

Category: Competition

Truth #6. A competitor will develop a less expensive product.

Background & Introduction. One might ask, "How do successful businesses get pushed out of markets they once dominated?" The theory of disruptive innovation explains how smaller businesses can disrupt incumbents by entering the bottom of a market with a low-cost business model. See how to expand and influence the marketplace using patterns of disruption in Figure 24. Disruptive Strategy states that there are three types of innovation:

1. **Sustaining innovation** is when a company creates better products to sell for higher profits to its best customers.
2. **Low-end disruption** is when a company enters the bottom of an existing market and offers a lower-priced product with acceptable performance, ultimately capturing its competitors' customers.
3. **New-market disruption** is when a company creates and claims a new segment in an existing market by catering to an underserved customer base. Then, quality slowly improves until the incumbent businesses' products are passé.

Low-end and new-market disruption are examples of disruptive innovation, differentiated by their relationships with the existing market.

New-market disruption occurs when an innovative product creates a new market segment. In contrast, low-end disruption enters at the bottom of the existing market to provide a "good enough" product to an overserved audience.

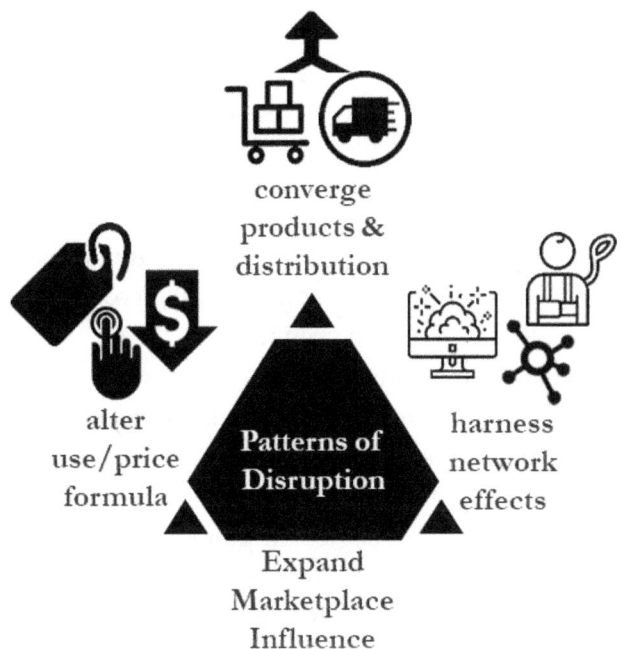

Figure 24: Patterns of Disruption to Look for to Expand the Marketplace

Understanding how disruption works can enable you to avoid it if you work at an incumbent business or drive it if you're a new entrant. Three characteristics separate low-end disruption from other innovation types:

- It offers "good enough" quality by market standards, but not the best. Customers at the top of the market likely won't be interested in this product, making it seem non-threatening to incumbent businesses.
- It targets consumers at the bottom of the market. The current product offerings overserve these people; they don't need all the bells and whistles with an expensive price tag.
- It profits at lower prices per unit sold than the incumbent businesses. This is essential because if the profit margins are lower than incumbents' products, they won't be motivated to fight the entrant for market share. The incumbent businesses' pursuit of profit is the causal mechanism that enables entrants to continue to move upmarket.

Purpose. This chapter describes how innovative disruption occurs when you or your competitor develops a less expensive product. It is impossible to anticipate when a rival introduces a cheaper product and grabs a portion of your market. However, there are actions that company leaders can take to improve their readiness to survive and thrive in an innovation disruption.

Challenge. The best way to understand what turns a new technology or approach into something cataclysmic to the marketplace is to do your due diligence. The goal is to avert disaster. (1) see it coming, (2) understand the shape new threats are likely to assume (patterns of disruption). Number three is to understand what disruptive strategies your market is most vulnerable to, and (4) understand what will act as catalysts for those threats. Consider the challenges in Figure 25. The challenge can be devastating; note three effects below:

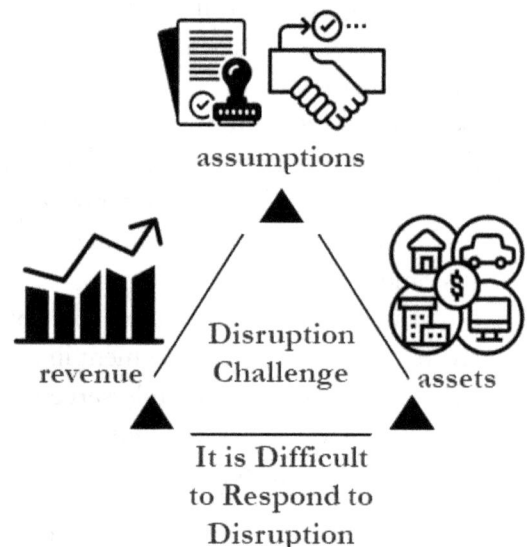

- Cannibalizes core revenue streams. Competing in a digital marketplace requires lower profit margins and erodes revenues from physical channels.
- Renders significant assets obsolete. Substantial investments in brick-and-mortar retail, manufacturing, and logistics facilities become less valuable.
- Challenges core assumptions. Changes assumptions about how much customers need physical facilities to make purchases.

This is the challenge that the decision maker faces when a competitor develops a less expensive product.

Figure 25: It is Difficult to Respond to a Disruptive Challenge

Solution. "How can I anticipate the unexpected threats that could devastate my business?" This is the question that gives organizational leaders nightmares. The leadership team fills the days with managing the expected, such as the things that can be controlled. Also, hiring the right talent, developing the right capabilities, getting resources to the right place at the right time, maintaining margin, growing revenues, and delighting customers.

These expected challenges are challenging enough. But what about the unexpected, the disruptive? Companies facing disruption will generally have three options available to them:

1. **Contain or exit.** A company facing a disruptive threat may cede the market where disruption will occur and find a more sustainable business or market. This action is the incumbent's choice, while it can still control the timing and process of exiting the market.
2. **Be the disruptor.** This is a problematic option for all the reasons given above for why incumbents often fail to respond to disruption. However, forewarned is forearmed. Each barrier to responding is more surmountable when an incumbent has advance notice of the future market dynamics, either to lend urgency to examining its core assumptions or to begin planning how to change existing assets and revenue streams.
3. **Undermine the disruptor.** By understanding the levers that make a given pattern likely in its market, an incumbent can choose a strategy of shaping the market and influencing the catalysts to make a particular form of disruption less likely. Each of these three actions is difficult and dependent on the context of the anticipated disruption and the unique capabilities of the incumbent to execute an option.

The first step is to formulate a disruption plan. It can be a chapter in an overall disruption strategy or a standalone document. Assign key members and provide resources and policy guidance. Next, gather information and capture data from your organization, competitors, industry, and the community. See Figure 26 for suggestions. Place markers to alert your team of outliers that raise a red flag for consideration.

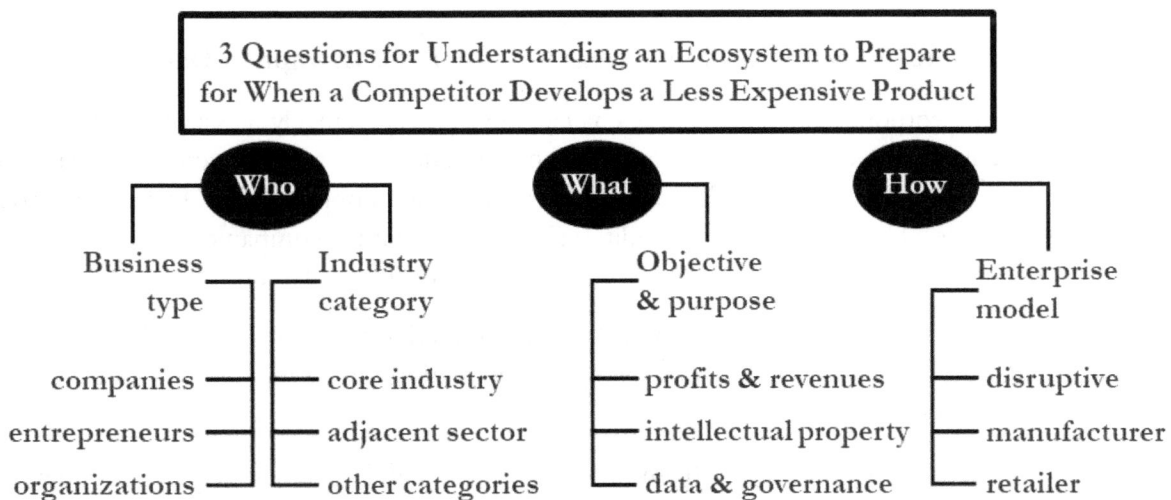

3 Questions for Understanding an Ecosystem to Prepare for When a Competitor Develops a Less Expensive Product

- **Who**
  - Business type
    - companies
    - entrepreneurs
    - organizations
  - Industry category
    - core industry
    - adjacent sector
    - other categories
- **What**
  - Objective & purpose
    - profits & revenues
    - intellectual property
    - data & governance
- **How**
  - Enterprise model
    - disruptive
    - manufacturer
    - retailer

Figure 26: Three Questions to Ask When Capturing Data to Prepare for Disruption

The solution is complex and sophisticated because you are trying to predict the future. However, by preparing, the organization can reduce the potential outlook for new products in a particular market. A small company may need more resources to collect information from all aspects of the marketplace. Still, even a few areas are healthy approaches when the industry erupts with activity. See Figure 27 for areas that may portend a disruption.

The next steps involve acting fast and having some automatic responses in place (public relations announcements, social media feeds, and a communications network that interconnects often).

Pieces of the puzzles come from many disparate sources. Interrogating diverse confidants (inside and outside the company) is an excellent policy.

When it comes to business strategy, "disruption" calls for a process in which market entrants come armed with non-conventional business models, and what at their outset seem to be poor-performing products (characterized as less expensive) come to challenge and eventually replace industry incumbents over time.

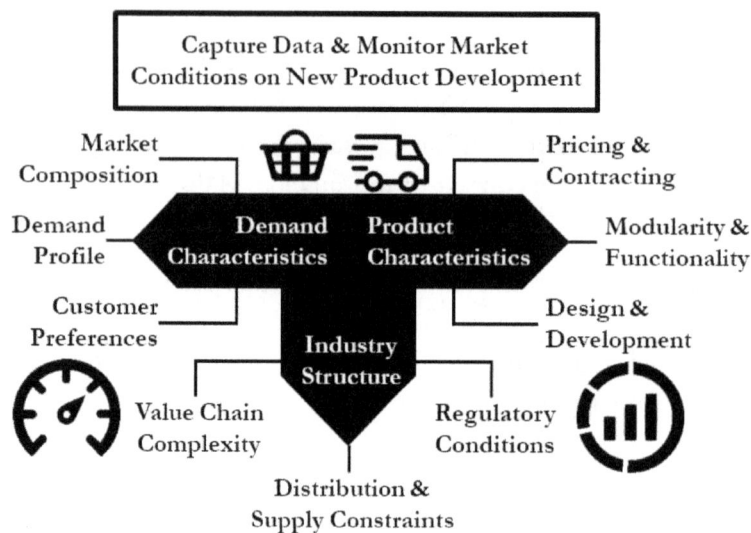

Figure 27: Business Model Areas to Explore for Disruption Data

Summary. Larger corporations find it tough, challenging, and yet strangely reassuring to take on familiar opponents whose ambitions, strategies, weaknesses, and even strengths resemble their own. CEOs can easily compare their game plans and prowess with their doppelgängers' by tracking stock prices by the minute. This obsession with traditional rivals has blinded companies to the threat of disruptive, low-cost competitors that enter the market with a less expensive product.

These examples offer nuggets of wisdom for both entrants and incumbents. Still, one lesson rings true for both: A foundation in the theory of disruptive innovation can be the difference between a business that survives and one that fails.

Whether you're approaching disruption from the perspective of an incumbent business or a new entrant, learning about types of disruptive innovation can enable you to craft strategies to prepare for or drive disruption.

References & Bibliography.

1. Catherine Cote, "What Is Low-End Disruption_ 2 Examples," HBS Online; January 13, 2022
2. "Disruptive Innovations - Christensen Institute," Christensen Institute," Christensen Institute; 2022
3. John Hagel, "Patterns-of-disruption: Anticipating disruptive strategies in a world of unicorns, black swans, and exponentials," Deloitte Insights; November 12, 2015
4. Catherine Cote, "What Is New Market Disruption_ 3 Examples," HBS Online; January 6, 2022
5. Nirmalya Kumar, "Strategies to Fight Low-Cost Rivals," HBS; December 12, 2006)

Category: Competition

Truth #7. You will be challenged by creative marketing.

Background & Introduction. More than just a buzzword, disruptive marketing changes how we react to, understand, and accept companies and their advertising. From a business standpoint, disruptive marketing represents a key shift in an era where promotional strategies update as fast as the technology that carries them.

Disruptive marketing is taking all the marketing rules and disturbing them. It turns your marketing plan and policies upside down. Disruptive marketing changes customer perceptions about the company and the industry. Customers love disruptive marketing because it changes the face of advertising. Customers want to buy, but they also want to be entertained.

Everyone knows the big winners in disruptive creative marketing, such as companies like Amazon, Uber, Red Bull, and Airbnb. However, consider thinking smaller. For example, Airwick captured much of the air freshener market by creating "The Scent Decorator." This simple variation to their existing collection of fresheners disrupted the market, and they grabbed market share.

Digital marketing disruption describes the change when new technologies, services, capabilities, and business models impact the value of the industry's existing services and goods and how they are marketed. These new disruptive tactics change or disrupt the sales process, forcing businesses to reevaluate their current market strategies regarding goods and services and possibly adjust their working concept.

History has many examples of superior technology supplanting the status quo. The automobile replaced the horse and buggy, electric lights replaced candles and oil lamps, mobile phones ended landline superiority, and video killed the radio star. The bottom line is that digital disruption means change, which can be good or bad. Figure 28 shows how to be ready for disruption at a macro level.

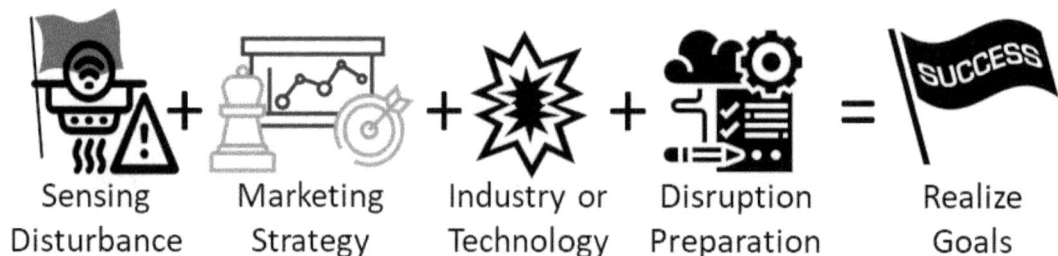

Sensing Disturbance + Marketing Strategy + Industry or Technology + Disruption Preparation = Realize Goals

Figure 28: Prepare for Creative Marketing Disruption

Purpose. Disruptive marketing doesn't have to break the bank to be effective. It must change how things are done – even a little. Disruptive brands don't just push the envelope; they crumple it and throw it in the trash. The purpose of this chapter is to discuss the means of coping with disruptive marketing tactics that impact your business.

Challenges. Disruptive innovation is a process rather than a product or service. Whether you're an incumbent intent on defending your market share and profits or a new entrant seeking to grab a slice of market share, understanding disruptive innovation as a process can offer valuable insights you can incorporate into your business plan. The disruptions you must worry about are the ones that genuinely threaten the organization. Understanding the correct meaning and application of "disruption" will help you identify and target actual threats. Knowing in advance or as soon as possible when disruption attacks your business. Also, it is achievable to have a plan to mitigate the impact, turn it around, and make it a success.

Description. Consider crafting a marketing-focused addition to your overall disruption plan to improve your readiness for managing creative market disruption. Figure 29 provides suggestions and a short process for sensing a coming disruption and reacting favorably.

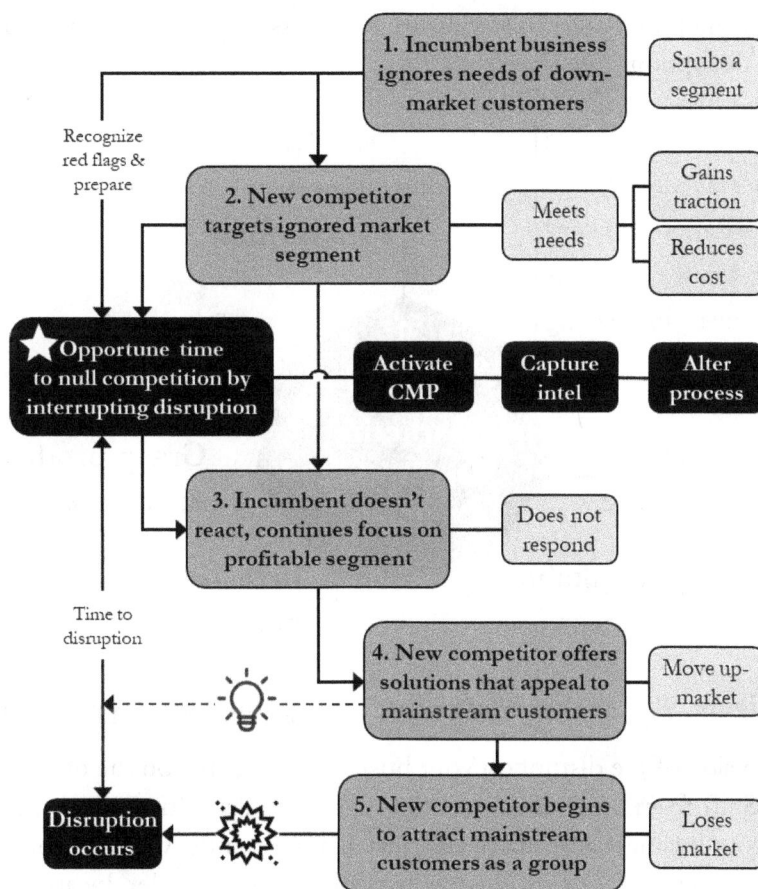

Figure 29: Creative Marketing Disruption Description

The figure shows five distinct events that occur to surprise the industry with a disruption. The successful business will sense a change, react, and turn it into a favorable outcome. See the list below.

1. Incumbent businesses innovate and develop their products or services to appeal to their most demanding and/or profitable customers, ignoring the needs of those down markets.
2. Entrants target this ignored market segment and gain traction by meeting their needs at a reduced cost compared to the incumbent's offerings.
3. Incumbents don't respond to the new entrant, focusing on their more profitable segments.
4. Entrants eventually move upmarket by offering solutions that appeal to the incumbent's "mainstream" customers.
5. Once the new entrant has begun to attract the incumbent business's mainstream customers as a group, disruption has occurred.

Disruption is broken down into four distinct elements, each with the potential to change a business approach to marketing. These are technology, business, industry, and society:

Solution. Prepare for disruption; this should be the mantra for the business to stay competitive during these fast-moving times. The following are readiness suggestions to consider when your organization senses disruption. See Figure 30.

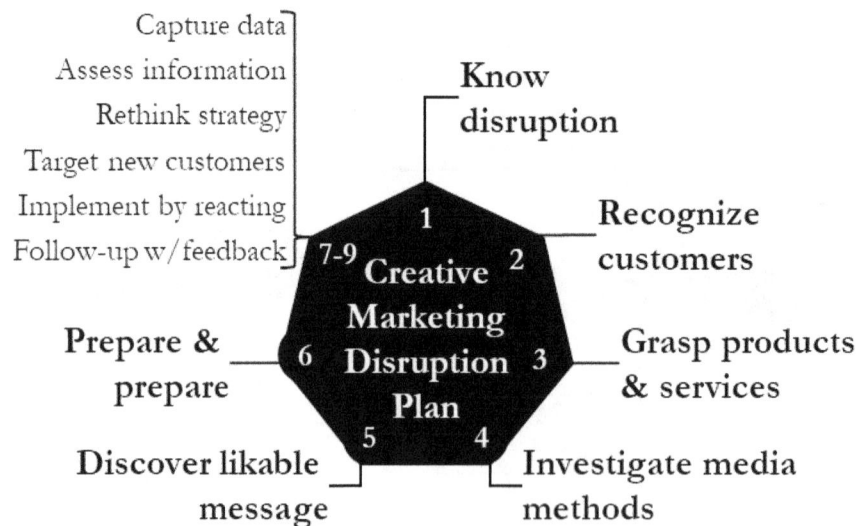

Figure 30: Creative Marketing Disruption Plan Suggestions

1. Know which side of the disruption your business is on; are you the disruptor or the disrupted? Shift from time-based decision-making to data-driven decision-making.
2. Recognize your business customers and, just as importantly, who are not your customers. Explore all demographics of the customer pool, e.g., age, gender, location, interests, etc.)
3. Understand the company's products and services from the customer's point of view. This includes the production methods and locations, as well as the entire supply chain.
4. Investigate all marketing avenues (traditional media & social media) and craft advertising to win the customer's appeal. Stay abreast of innovative technologies and global phenomena.

5. Discover a way for consumers to purchase products and services with a bonus: enjoy the message. Consumers identify with products that make them feel positive.
6. Accomplish as much preparation as possible ahead of time. At a minimum, assign the task to an able person ahead of time, like a "disruption director." A disruption team is always a good idea. Their duties may be minimal (additional), but they keep the business current, focused on marketing, and plugged into the world.
7. Constantly capture data and information, regularly evaluate and redesign marketing strategy, target new customers, and frequently change the marketing approach when it becomes stale.
8. Implement disruption or discover disturbance and react. Record lessons learned, talk about experiences, and provide instruction.
9. Follow-up, collect feedback during each phase, then use it.

Summary. Creative marketing disruption is a phrase that has been used in the marketing world for more than 15 years to describe the desired break in existing patterns of behavior of the target audience in response to a highly creative message (advertising). "Disruption" signals a departure from the norm. Disruptive messaging disrupts the mediocrity in the deluge of advertising the consumer encounters.

The savvy business finds an innovative way to pause the potential consumer long enough to gain their interest in your product or service. Disruption can't be a one-time endeavor. The ability to disrupt and sense disruption is a learned agility that helps continuously evolve your business.

Creative marketing often uses ingenious means to engage consumers and initiate two-way conversations. This ability enables a disruptive marketing trend. Rising to this challenge will bring rewards beyond direct sales. These rewards are generated in consumer content based on authentic brand engagements and newfound relationships. The benefit is sharing this content via social media and realizing maximum return on engagement.

References & Bibliography.

1. "These Disruptive Marketing Examples Will Inspire You," Elevate; March 7, 2018
2. Chris Larson, "What Is Disruptive Innovation Theory 4 Key Concepts," HBS Online; August 30, 2019
3. Sherice Jacob, "4 Ways Disruptive Marketing is Winning Over Customers," Patel blog; 2022
4. "What Is Digital Disruption and the Top Five Digital Disruptors to Watch Out for in 2022," Simplilearn; April 2022
5. "Creative disruption," Wikipedia; 2022
6. Building a habit of disruption in marketing," McKinsey; April 29, 2019

Category: Personnel
Truth #8. Health issues will affect your employees.

Background & Introduction. The health and well-being of a company's workforce are critical to survival in the competitive business world. Vibrant and energetic employees are essential to prepare for any disruption. The recent pandemic has taught all organizations this lesson many times. Preparing for a health disruption that will affect employee behavior and, ultimately, the business operation is crucial. Several experts have researched and shown that a workplace can proactively upgrade employee health by offering exercise memberships, healthy snack and lunch options, first-class medical plans, and paid vacation. However, combined mental and physical health is just as important and requires attention.

Disruption is a part of life, and business leaders today are paid to make decisions in the gray zone, where certainty is scarce. However, leaders can navigate complex times better by using the correct response when faced with an uncertain future. A well-planned strategy for disruption can become a cultural strength in the workplace. See Figure 31.

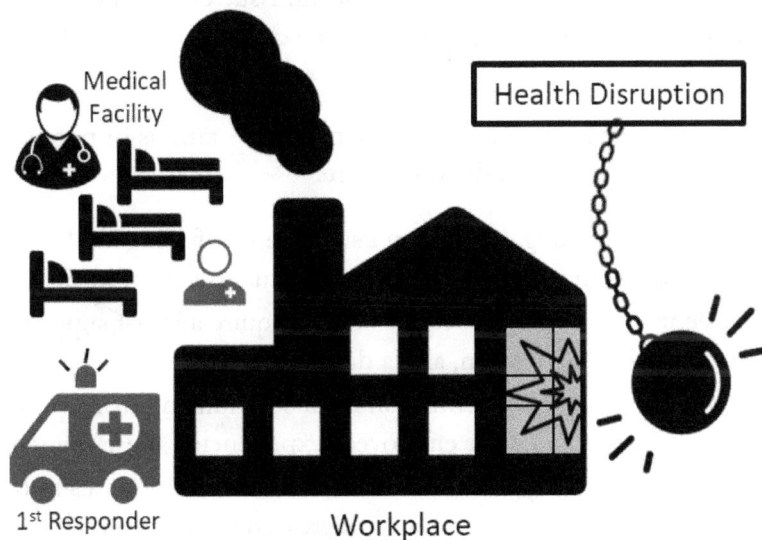

Figure 31: Workplace Health Disruption

Few employees strongly agree that their organization's leadership makes them enthusiastic about the future, and only 13% strongly agree their leadership communicates effectively. Therefore, most workers are even less prepared for a health disruption than their leaders. Figure 31 illustrates that a Health disruption causes chaos and arrives with a bang.

Purpose. The purpose of this chapter is to describe an approach to preparing for a health disruption that is severe enough to affect a company's employee behaviors. The discussion presents several graphics outlining a health and wellness program that anticipates a pandemic-like event that impacts the workforce, the workplace, and most business operations. The resulting outcomes affect employee behaviors for months and years to come and may change how work is completed in the future. The long-term effects on employee well-being cost the companies millions in lost revenue, health costs, and employee production.

Challenge. While all enterprises have different needs and situations, some fundamental underlying principles of a healthy workplace initiative will raise its likelihood of success. These principles are significant before, during, and after a workplace health disruption. They are:

- Leadership engagement based on core values
- Involve workers and their representatives
- Gap analysis: measure the difference between before and after
- Learn from others: call upon subject matter experts
- Sustainability: healthy workplace initiatives are integrated
- Importance of integration: engage diverse workers

Business leadership faces the challenge of preparing for health disruptions that affect workforce behaviors. To do so, they must prepare the leadership, prepare the employees, gather the resources, and develop a reasonable plan to survive and recover from a health disruption event.

Description. Planning for a health disruption differs from sudden types of disruption, such as weather, terrorism, or natural disasters. A disruptive health issue takes time to develop, and much of the recovery time dwells on the "return to normal." Some of the physical and mental concerns are shown in Figure 32.

Psychological effects that emerge as the most prominent manifestations of people experiencing work-related stress due to a health-related disruption are:

- Depression: employees battling depression usually report feeling aimless, tired, restless, and experiencing low morale; they hide their symptoms due to fear of losing their jobs.
- Anxiety: anxious employees with anxiety disorders require a lot of support, low morale, irritability, an increase in absenteeism, and a drop in productivity.
- Loss of Concentration: loss of concentration results in human errors, poor decision-making, low productivity, and low morale for employees experiencing these mental health issues.
- Changes in Behavior (Irritability, restlessness, nervousness): Pressures in the workplace may cause people to develop nervous attitudes or decreased patience levels.
- Physical Symptoms (shoulder, back, and neck): for people battling mental health issues, physical symptoms sometimes can be indicative of deeper psychological problems.

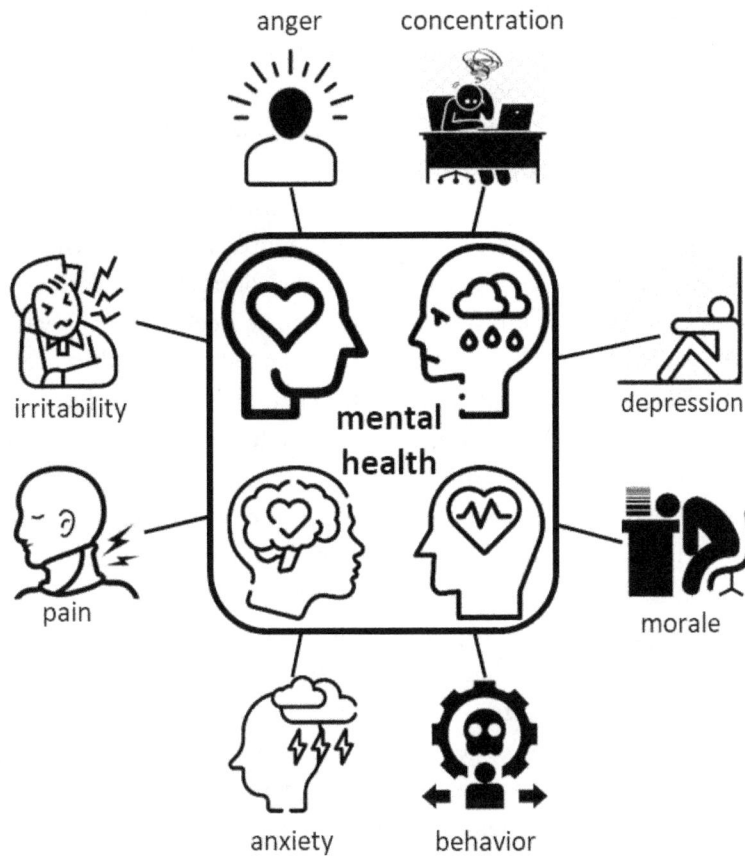

Figure 32: Mental Health is Often Overlooked as Workplace Behavior Driver

There's a lot of concentration on the factory floor to oiling machines and putting sensors on machines to ensure they're operating well, but businesses often don't do that with people. They ask if people have IT support. But really, organizations need to think deeper than that. What signals does the workforce emit for the business leadership to realize something is amiss? One thing a company can do is devise and pilot programs to improve workplace resilience and connectedness. See Figure 33 to begin.

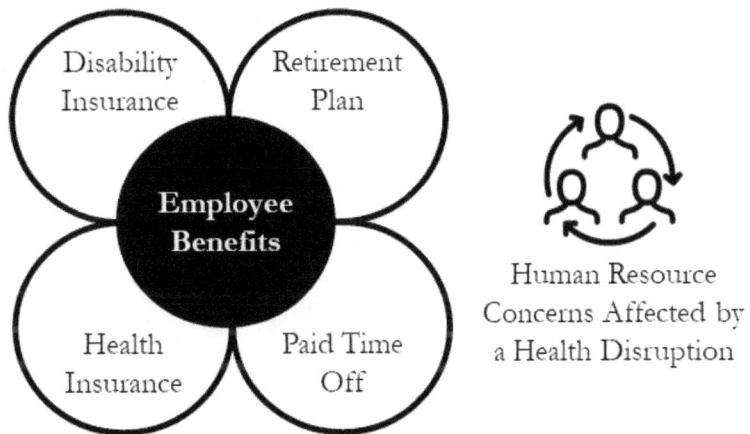

Figure 33: The Human Resources Department is a Good Place to Start

Solution. The World Health Organization recommends the steps listed below as a beginning to preparation for a health disruption.

1. **Mobilize.** Mobilizing employers and workers to invest in change will be critical to building commitment around an action or initiative involving health disruption response.
2. **Assemble.** Assemble a healthy workplace team and conserve resources to implement a particular change in the workplace to improve health awareness for all employees. See Figure 34 for a plan to maintain ethics and values.
3. **Assess.** The health disruption team captures available organization data. It establishes a baseline on workplace inspections, prior hazard identification and risk assessment processes, health and safety committee minutes, employee demographics, turnover, and productivity statistics. Collect workers' health information such as occupational health data, rates of sick leave and workplace-related injuries and illnesses, and short- and long-term disabilities.
4. **Prioritize.** Prioritize team actions by considering a diverse set of factors. These factors include occupational hazard exposure, workplace safety risks, company policies and directives, and the cost of doing nothing.
5. **Plan.** Develop a health disruption plan as part of the overall health program. Focus on a few of the priorities identified as most critical to health and goals most readily attainable, with an indication of time frames.
6. **Do.** Take decisive action on the list of measures identified. Assign responsibilities to various members within the implementation team and follow up as needed.
7. **Evaluate.** Evaluate and measure the health disruption program as it progresses. Compare outcomes to the baseline knowledge gathered in step 3 (Assess). Track these numbers, look for trends, and compare them to previous benchmarks.
8. **Improve.** Seeking to improve health and well-being is a continuous process. Look outside the organization for lessons learned from similar experiences for ideas that enhance the health disruption program.

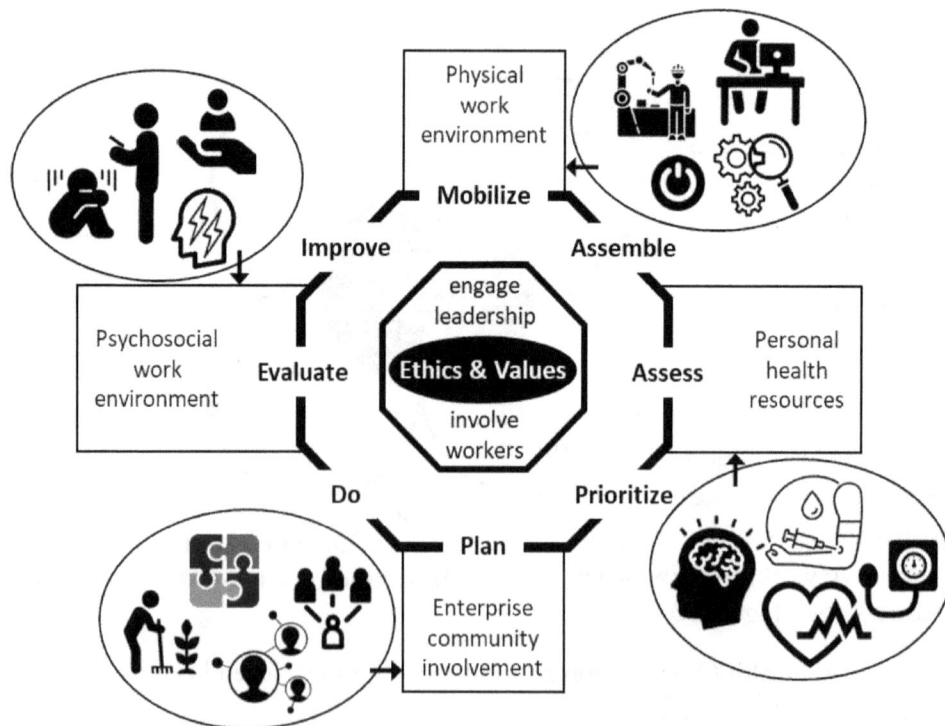

Figure 34: Prepare for Health Disruption by Maintaining Ethics & Values

The definition of health is a state of complete physical, mental, and social well-being and not merely the absence of disease. A healthy workplace is one in which workers and managers collaborate to use a continual improvement process to protect and promote the health, safety, and well-being of all workers and the sustainability of the workplace.

Summary. To create a healthy workplace and prepare for a health disruption, an organization needs to consider the available knowledge of the company, community, and stakeholders that influence where actions can best take place and the most effective processes by which employers and workers can execute and implement a health disruption plan.

References & Bibliography.

1. "How to reduce the pandemic impact on employees," Deloitte Insights; October 22, 2020
2. Alvin Powell, "Disruption of work relationships adds to mental-health concern," Harvard Gazette; September 25, 2020
3. Vibhas Ratanjee and Stephanie Barrymore, "What Leaders Can Do to Prepare for Disruption," Gallup Workplace; February 20, 2019
4. Kelly Greenwood and Julia Anas, "It's a New Era for Mental Health at Work," Harvard Business Review; October 4, 2021
5. Ward van Zoonen and Claartje ter Hoeven, "Disruptions and General Distress for Essential and Nonessential Employees," April 1, 2021
6. "Workplace Violence – Overview," Occupational Safety and Health Administration; 2022
7. Martin Tušl, Rebecca Brauchli, Philipp Kerksieck, and Georg Friedrich Bauer, "Impact of the COVID-19 crisis on work and private life, mental well-being and self-rated health in German and Swiss employees: a cross-sectional online survey," BMC Public Health; 2021
8. "Healthy workplaces: a model for action," World Health Organization; 2022
9. Hayley Shaughnessy, "Disruption in the Workplace," Monster.ca; 2022
10. "Workplace Disruption and the Future of Work_ 2025 Is the New 2030," ASUG; March 26, 2021
11. Phillip Wilson, "Viewpoint: 6 Steps for Responding Properly to Workplace Disruptions," SHRM; July 10, 2018
12. Ghassan Khoury and Jeremie Brecheisen, "The Future of Work Means Managing Through Disruption," Gallup Workplace; September 20, 2019
13. Jennifer Stone, "Mental Health in the Workplace: Psychological Effects and Support!" RTOR Gateway to Mental Health Services; December 18, 2019
14. "Mental Health and Substance Use," World Health Organization; 2022

Category: Personnel

Truth #9. Employee turnover will occur.

Background & Introduction. Global economies are constantly changing, and preparing for change is always challenging. This topic applies to every business with at least one employee.

It's not a revelation that high employee turnover can devastate any company. Whether it be direct replacement costs like recruiting, interviewing, and onboarding or indirect costs like lost productivity, damaged client relationships, decreased revenue, and lowered employee morale, the total cost of turnover can be massive.

High turnover rates can negatively affect a company and its employees. The constant need to hire and train new employees makes it easy to veer from the organization's mission and vision. By retaining employees, companies can provide a higher-caliber workforce that positively affects the bottom line. Businesses can lower turnover rates by providing adequate training, rewarding employees for a job well done, and creating a company culture of trust. See Figure 35.

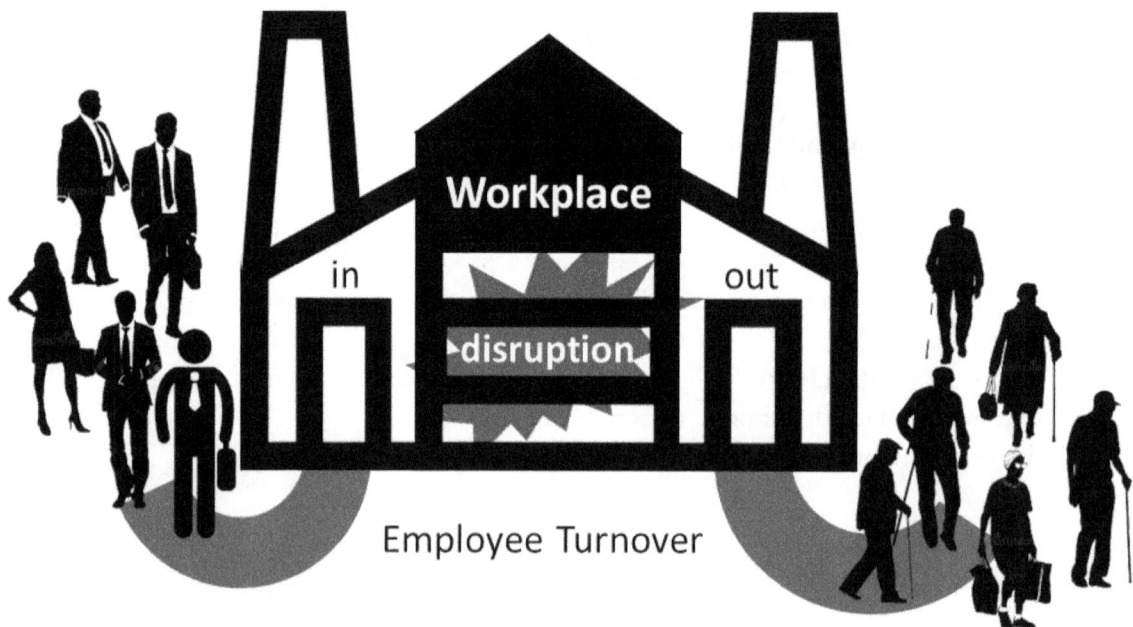

Figure 35: Employee Turnover Disruption Including Older Workers

Purpose. This chapter provides a methodology and framework to improve an organization's readiness for a disruption caused by employee turnover, including senior management. The chapter describes the challenge and proposed solution. It also describes the drivers and reasons for disruptive employee turnover that can harm a business in the near and long term. Finally, it proposes the CERTIFY process as an outstanding approach to becoming prepared beforehand to solve and mitigate the chaos resulting from employee turnover disruption.

Challenge. The biggest challenge when it comes to turnover is identifying the root cause(s) of the problem. Companies spend hundreds of thousands of dollars monitoring employee engagement, adding expensive company perks, training managers, etc., assuming such efforts will help reduce their turnover. The reality is that although these methods have merit, other drivers behind high turnover exist.

Most voluntary turnover is caused by people seeking—in no particular order—more money, better benefits, an improved work/life balance, more opportunities to progress in their careers, time to address personal issues like health problems or relocations, increased flexibility, or to escape a toxic or ineffective manager or workplace. See Figure 36.

Solution. High employee turnover is costly and disruptive but avoidable.

Experts cite offering competitive pay and benefits and maintaining a healthy company culture as two essential employee retention strategies.

Studies reveal that employees also value the opportunity to grow on the job. An organization should provide opportunities for growth and development.

Offering employees opportunities for growth and development makes good business sense. This benefits both the employee and the organization.

So, how can an organization best provide growth opportunities for employees? Learning and development – often referred to as reskilling or upskilling– is the answer.

Figure 36: Employee Turnover Drivers

Upskilling refers to taking skills and knowledge to a new level and is primarily focused on helping employees become more skilled and relevant in their current positions within the organization. Reskilling, on the other hand, refers to learning new skills for a different job.

Both reskilling and upskilling are key to employee growth and retention. Ensuring that employees continuously learn, adapt, and acquire new skills allows organizations to avoid many financial pitfalls associated with high turnover.

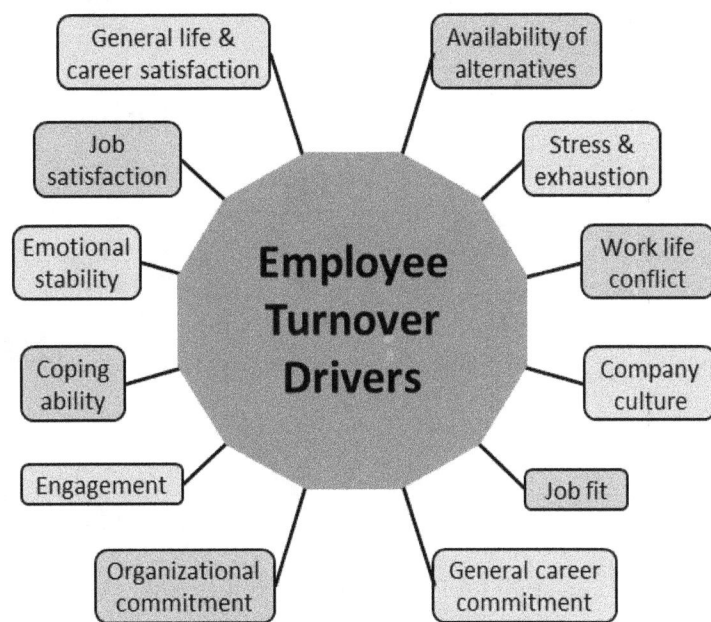

Retain older workers; they are a significant asset. Delaying retirement means companies have additional time to identify a worker's key proficiencies and ensure the knowledge is transferred to younger employees to prevent future skills gaps. While older workers can be more expensive, they can usually ease into retirement, have more flexible hours, and are more productive with their skills.

Description. Businesses have unique challenges with each workforce. Some reasons why the workforce can be displeased are provided in Figure 37. Some straightforward actions that an organization can adopt are listed below—all part of creating a healthy workplace culture.

- Gather data from all facets of the hiring and employee retention process
- Screen new hires for turnover
- Provide competitive salary, benefits, and work safety
- Create and maintain a healthy culture
- Value the opportunity to grow on the job
- Have HR conduct an anonymous exit interview
- Understand the nuances of turnover: age, career, geography, pay, culture, gender, & others.
- Benchmark employee retention rate, cost of employee turnover, and data collection are significant parts of the CERTIFY process.

Employee Turnover Reasons

Lack of purpose | Poor compensation | Being overworked | Bad managers | No feedback

Bad hiring procedures | No growth opportunity | Toxic culture | Boredom | Poor work-life balance

Figure 37: Employee Turnover Reasons

Actions. Many recommendations that an organization can begin right now and incorporate into its company culture, mission statement, and belief system to maintain and attract talented employees are listed below. The CERTIFY process will provide a comprehensive structure for addressing employee turnover disruption. Two formulas a company should be regularly computing are also in the list below. See Figure 38 for an overview of the CERTIFY process.

1. Turnover Rate for Given Period = Number of Separations / Avg. Number of Employees x 100%

2. Cost of turnover = # departures x average cost of departures
3. By redefining who you are as a business, update your company's culture.
4. By engineering new and creative ways to fulfill employee wants, needs, and demands in today's growing, evolving, complex world.
5. Convey the urgency of this change. We feel it's critical to every business's growth and development.
6. Leverage the technology and build an ecosystem to engage and support your workforce that works for them today.
7. Promoting a work/life balance and productivity is a top priority.
8. For the older workforce, offer flexible scheduling options, recognize mature workers, consider a variety of mentoring match-ups, and provide ongoing learning opportunities.

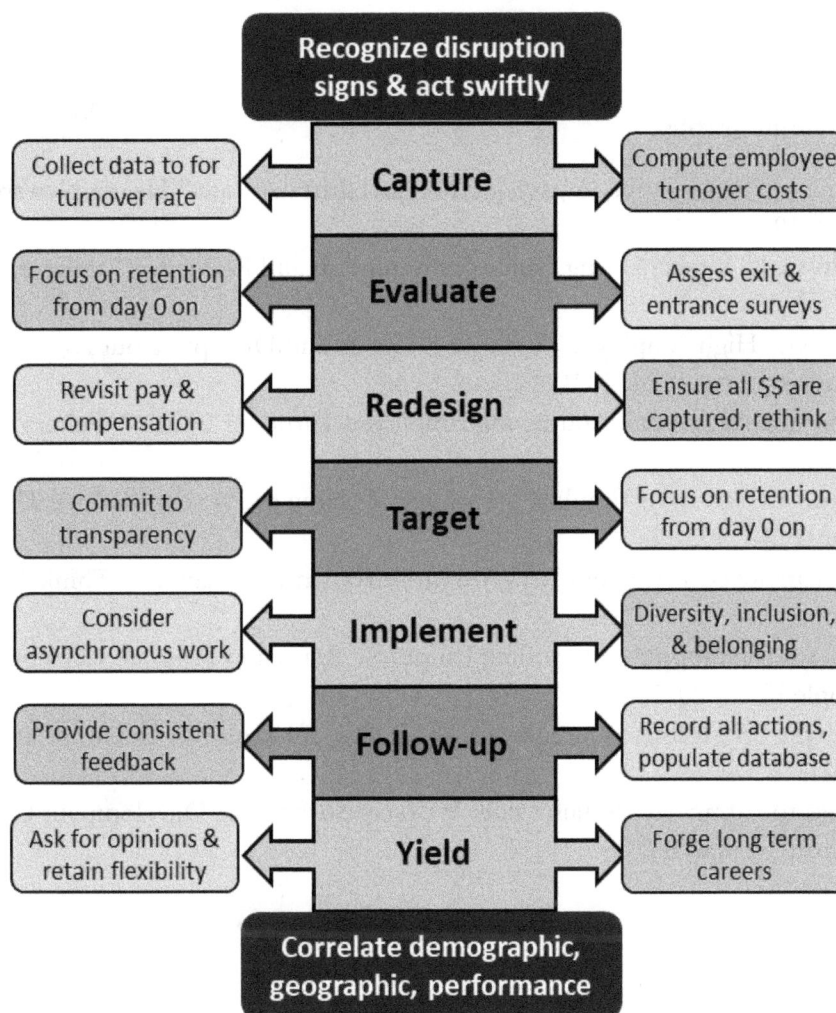

Figure 38: The CERTIFY Methodology as it Relates to Employee Turnover Disruption

Summary. An employee turnover disruption (by definition) will be a surprise. But your plan of attack should already be prepared. Your organization will be judged on how it responds. You'll need a disruption plan and a disruption response team. You must read the signs, react swiftly, and prepare yourself and your organization.

The most crucial step is to measure your progress against turnover on a per-hire basis – specifically about the attributes you've screened for.

For companies with high turnover, the most important thing to take away from the discussion is that your screening plan for identifying great candidates must include retention-related criteria. You can hire the most superb performer on the planet, but they aren't successful if they leave your company after only one month.

The second most important thing to take away from this chapter is that when it comes to reducing turnover in hiring, data is your greatest ally. Reducing turnover in hiring will require being deliberate about what you're screening for and why you're screening for it – and being willing to collect data as you go so that you can continuously improve over time. Utilize the CERTIFY methodology to get started.

References and Bibliography.

1. Miki Markovich, "The Negative Impacts of a High Turnover Rate," Hearst Newspapers; February 04, 2019
2. Dr. John Sullivan, "Ultimate Hiring Guide for Retention and Reducing Turnover," Journey Front; 2022
3. Norine Wiebmer, "High Employee Turnover is Costly and Disruptive but Avoidable," NWI Business Solutions; August 24, 2021
4. Nikki Nelson, "Identifying and Addressing Employee Turnover Issues," Walters & Kluwer; January 7, 2021
5. Marc Holliday, "10 Causes of Employee Turnover & How to Prevent/Reduce Them," Oracle NetSuite; January 14, 2021
6. Josh Purvis, "Employee Turnover Costs Are More Expensive Than You Think," Assembly; March 7, 2022
7. "11 Strategies for Building an Outstanding Employee Retention Program On a Small Business Budget," People Keep; 2021
8. Michelle Graham, "A Holistic White Paper: The 5 W's of Employee Retention in 2021," Click Boarding; 2021
9. "Creative Ways to Attract and Retain Older Workers Sustainable Development Goals - Resource Centre," 5 March 2019

Category: Personnel

Title: #10. Skillsets Will Become Outdated.

Background & Introduction. Imagine yourself as a veteran employee who has worked hard for the company for 15-20 years. You've been a model employee. You are very skilled at your job. The company is undergoing a technology refresh or upgrade to become more competitive. The result is that your skillset is no longer required to produce or contribute to the company's core competency. The company has asserted that your expertise has become obsolescent. What happens? If this happens to several employees and skill sets, the company is experiencing a disruption. An abrupt transformation is required to keep the company afloat. This chapter exposes this challenge to businesses choosing to modernize regarding technology, digital finance, and environmental requirements. To compete, the company needs a different skill set; another employee group needs to be hired or trained to meet this demand. This is not a new topic but is fast rising in interest because of the speed at which this trend is happening. Thereby escalating to the level of disruption. See Figure 39.

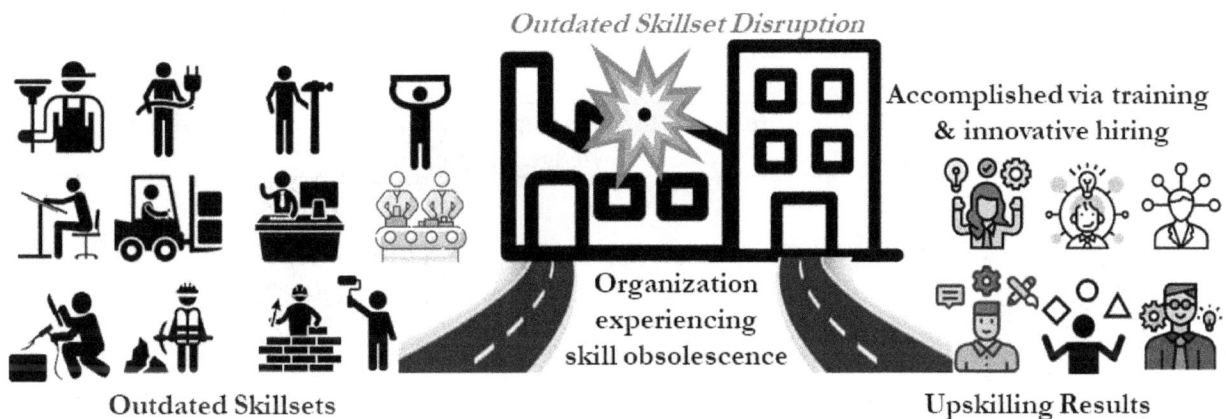

Figure 39: Outdated Skillsets Cause Disruption

Skills obsolescence results from industrial restructuring or changing skill needs in technologically intensive sectors and occupations, which may render workers' skills outdated. It can also arise as adults' physical and cognitive skills and abilities deteriorate with age due to atrophy or wear and tear. Individuals and employers must commit to continuous adult learning to prevent skills obsolescence.

Purpose. Adversity can often be a force for rapid change and for societies to advance. Digital transformation is occurring at an unprecedented pace – creating jobs and driving sweeping change with the potential to improve people's lives and create a more connected world. Today, technology breakthroughs are driving mass training programs, workforce transformation, and demanding flexibility. In addition, employees call for a better work-life blend, more upskilling, and greater autonomy over how, when, and where work gets done. These results are all welcome upsides of disruption. The purpose of this chapter is to discuss a methodology for a company facing skillset obsolescence and assist in preparing for disruption.

Challenges. Company shareholders do not want to carry an out-of-date workforce. Employers want to refrain from paying employees to learn. They want to hire people who add value from day one. That is a challenge on several levels, as the workforce does not exist instantaneously, is not geographically available, and may not be relevant environmentally. Also, the lack of upskilling opportunities disproportionately affects populations who are already vulnerable today. These workers most likely fill many low-skill jobs that will soon be fully automated. Without addressing this need, we are headed toward a future of increasing inequality. This, coupled with the personnel transformation required through hiring, training, and/or a blend of both, can be daunting. Not least of which is the required timeliness. To attempt to portray several aspects of this challenge, explore the age segments and preferences of the U.S. potential workforce in Table 3.

Group	Birth Years	Characteristic
Baby Boomers	1951-1964	Hold the most social capital, transitioned to remote work most successfully
Generation X	1965-1980	Financially the most stressed segment, caring for children & aging parents
Millennials/Generation Y	1981-1994	Most focused on what their work/life balance looks like, less connected to coworkers
Generation Z	1995-2009	Seek employer cares about philanthropy & social issues; also core values, purpose &transparency
Generation Alpha	2010-Present	Growing up in a digital environment, with all knowledge just a click away

Table 3: U.S. Population Segments of Potential Workers

Solution. The challenge is to prepare for disruption. Redefining the company's skills framework is a good start. Recent research and job reports show that several critical professional skill clusters are emerging. These reflect the adoption of new technologies—giving rise to the demand for green economy jobs, roles at the forefront of the data and Artificial Intelligence (AI) economy, and new roles in Industrial Internet of Things (IIoT) engineering, cloud computing, and product development. The future of work shows demand for a wide variety of skills that match these professional opportunities, including disruptive technical skills, specialized industry skills, and core business skills. Consider creating a skills tree. See Figure 40.

Description. The growing interdependence of human and technical skills is only one factor that demands new skill-development frameworks. The only way to prepare for skill obsolescence is to have a Skill Transformation Plan (STP). Studies suggest that skills generally have a period of usefulness of about five years, with more technical skills at just two and a half years. The short shelf-life of technical skills requires a continuous re-skilling effort to stay relevant. According to the Chief Learning Officer Magazine, business leaders and learners need a completely new model for thinking about skills, a model that fosters thinking about emerging questions. The company's STP must address these topics and prepare as much as possible to survive this disruption.

There are many ways to describe skills. There are "soft" skills (skills that are universal and not associated with a particular job or industry – such as communications and collaboration) and "hard" skills (skills related to technical abilities typically acquired through formal education – such as coding or product knowledge). Employees at all levels need professional skills, regardless of their job role. Leadership skills are necessary for people to lead well. Occupational or technical skills are the skills that people need to perform specific tasks in their career fields.

Some critical skills are necessary today but will become obsolete within a few years. How do you balance durable and perishable skills in your workforce?

Perishable skills are specific technology skills updated frequently; organization-specific policies, tools, and specialized processes can all be classified as perishable.

Semi-durable skills tend to be frameworks with base knowledge from which field-specific technologies, processes, and tools arise. Figure 40 offers a generic example; each company will have a unique skills tree.

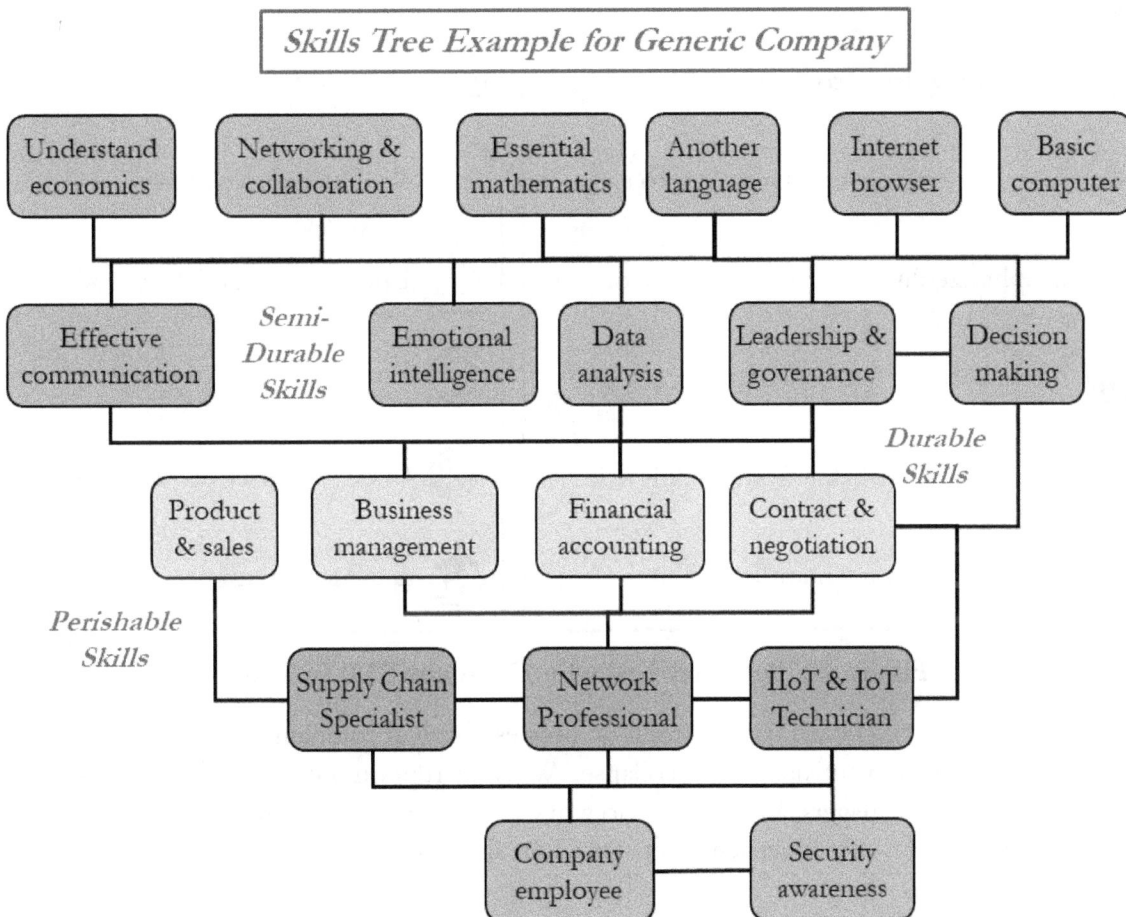

Figure 40: Skills Tree Example

Durable skills constitute a base layer of lifelong learning, mindsets, and dispositions. They include skills like design thinking, project management practices, effective communication, and leadership, which are more foundational.

As organizations and individuals prepare for a reset and start to consider a skills refresh, it's essential to consider just how transferable a given set of skills is. This, along with the durability of the skills, provides a framework that can adapt to changing business needs—building a skills tree.

While training people on perishable skills provides a quick ROI, it allows little flexibility between roles and job families. Approaching training from a durable-skills-first perspective empowers individuals to make dynamic, longer-term contributions to an organization as they navigate various jobs. Following a tree-shaped model may be a more effective way of thinking through skill development and bringing together an individual's skills, learning, and career.

Actions. The most important course of action is for the company to recognize the importance of preparing for disruption caused by outdated skills. Figure 41 provides some suggested considerations to include in their skillset transformation plan. Learning takes time.

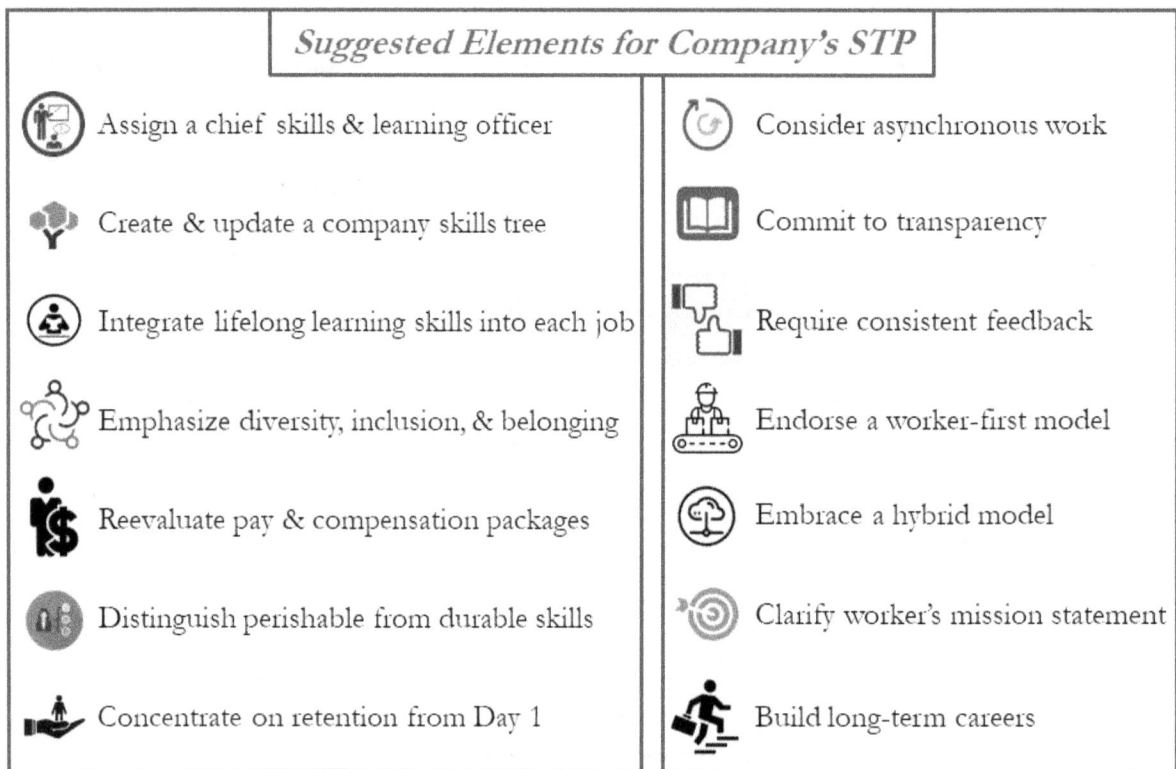

Suggested Elements for Company's STP

- Assign a chief skills & learning officer
- Create & update a company skills tree
- Integrate lifelong learning skills into each job
- Emphasize diversity, inclusion, & belonging
- Reevaluate pay & compensation packages
- Distinguish perishable from durable skills
- Concentrate on retention from Day 1
- Consider asynchronous work
- Commit to transparency
- Require consistent feedback
- Endorse a worker-first model
- Embrace a hybrid model
- Clarify worker's mission statement
- Build long-term careers

Figure 41: Potential Tasks for Company STP Inclusion

Summary. Disruption scholars have focused on how established companies, complacent in their industry position, need to anticipate their collapse. When disruption puts a company at risk, it also threatens the leaders, managers, and others who work for it. That exacerbates the problem because their insight is precisely what is needed. Get started on an STP.

References & Bibliography.

1. Stephanie Thurrott, "12 old-school skills that are becoming obsolete," Considerable; 11/21/20
2. Paul Heltzel , "6 dead-end IT skills — and how to avoid becoming obsolete," CIO; July 19, 2021
3. "Four outdated skills that aren't skills (unless they are)," Career Beacon; August 26, 2020
4. "Skills Revolution Reboot: The 3Rs - Renew, Reskill, Redeploy," The Findings; 2021
5. "New report lists the skills you'll need in 5 years," Career Beacon; December 10, 2020
6. Scott Engler, "Lack of Skills Threatens Digital Transformation," Gartner: July 21, 2020
7. Sonia Malik, "Skills Transformation for 2021 Workplace - IBM Blog," IBM; December 7, 2020
8. Mark Bonchek, "How to Stop Worrying about Becoming Obsolete at Work," HBR; 1/11/2016
9. "Understanding Durable vs. Perishable Skills and How to Balance Them," Avilar; June 16, 2021

Category: Personnel

Title: #11. Senior management and/or ownership will change.

Background & Introduction. We accept that changes are a fact of life. Significant changes we can't control or have little influence over are called disruptions today. You may have experienced a disruption in your organization through a leadership change. The owner sells the company, the chief executive officer signs up with a new business, and/or a key engineer with special skill/knowledge or intellectual collateral dies. The organization is now faced with significant change: does it fold, what happens to the workforce, who owns the assets, and what can the business entity do? It now becomes scary and chaotic. Life is often unpredictable, but we can prepare for leadership disruption in many ways.

Business owners sometimes encounter life-changing experiences such as heart attacks, cancer, or close calls to death in accidents. We all experience the death of parents, spouses, and friends. Such events can trigger significant changes in the desire to own and manage a business. Figure 42 identifies a few of the reasons that a company changes leadership.

Figure 42: Examples of Ways an Organization Can Change Leadership

The technical side of the change is undoubtedly complex. The company must work out the financial arrangements of the deal, integrate business systems, make decisions about the new organization's structure, and more. However, getting people on board and participating in the leadership change can make the difference between success and failure. Why? Individuals will need to perform their jobs differently. Often, a new set of mid-managers arrives with new ways of doing things.

The degree to which the workforce must change their behaviors and adopt new processes significantly impacts the outcome. Communication, perceptions, and openness are keys to mitigating disruptive leadership change as much as possible. It is essential to have completed planning for handling these uncertainties when they occur.

Purpose. The purpose of this chapter is to provide steps that an organization can complete beforehand to prepare for disruption. This chapter discusses the occurrence, effects, options, and impact that can happen during this period. It also provides suggestions for businesses to consider when preparing their company for this eventuality.

Challenges. In business, changing leadership abruptly means changing the company's ownership. A smaller company might be acquired by a larger one that believes that when the two are combined, they will be a more impressive competitor in the marketplace. Another perspective is that the company squanders profits, finds the workforce in disarray, loses its suppliers, and destroys its reputation within the community. See Figure 43.

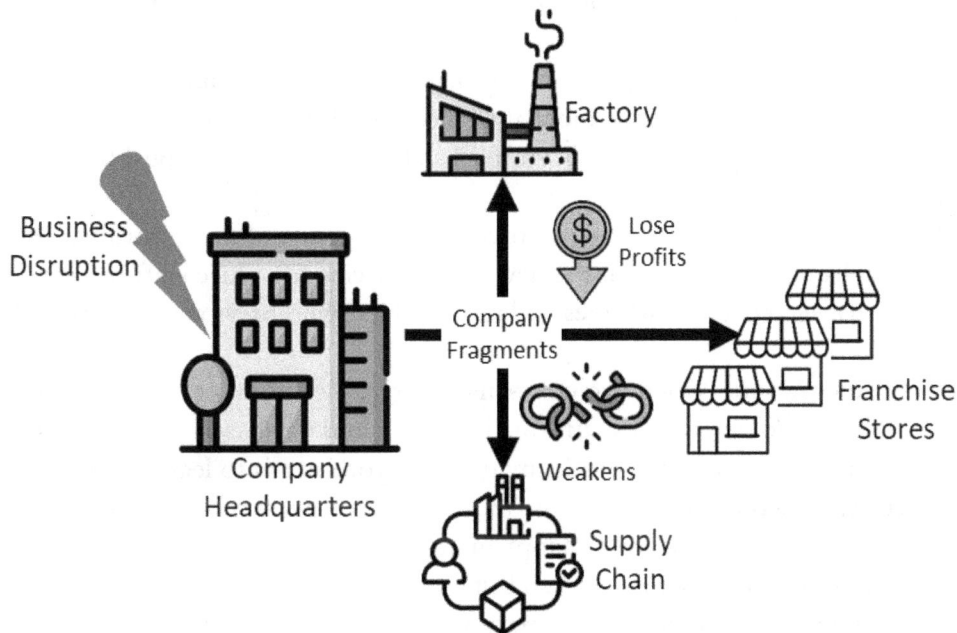

Figure 43: Possibilities Resulting from Disruptive Leadership Change

A sudden change in ownership also brings other changes to the organization that affect employees, suppliers, and customers. Preparation for this certainty needs to be completed upfront. The mantra to prepare for disruption should include this situation. Thus, the challenge is to include unexpected leadership changes in the organization's disruption planning.

The parallel challenge is to be alert for those positive factors that enable your organization to leverage a leadership change into a lucky success. New leadership can bring new talent, ideas, and funding. Thus, new products can be created and marketed. If the new product or service qualifies as disruptive, the new organization can quickly capture most of the market. We only need to consider Amazon, Uber, Airbnb, and Starbucks.

Preparing for disruptions will increase the likelihood of successfully transitioning a business through ownership or senior management change. An ownership change can be highly disruptive for an organization. Companies often need help meeting their financial goals, which can even endanger survival. It is traumatic, even if you're the seller. You want to ensure the business legacy lives on, the workforce is alright, and that suppliers and customers are cared for.

Description. An ownership/management transformation is complicated. Several moving parts require coordination. A few are listed below. Figure 44 provides a graphic depicting the potential impacts of this type of disruption.

a. **Change in Management Style.** A company's new owners will have a different management style than the previous ones, which means an adjustment period for employees, suppliers, and customers.

b. **Reorganization.** A change in business ownership often brings about changes to the organizational structure. Management at all levels needs to practice good communications, be transparent, attempt to get buy-in from all stakeholders, look for pushback, and mitigate as best you can.

c. **Personnel Changes.** From the workforce standpoint, one of the unfortunate outcomes of a business changing hands is that the new owners decide to reduce staff or bring in their people in management or staff roles and replace those who previously occupied those positions.

d. **Systems Integration.** When two companies merge, they often need help integrating their information technology systems, information flows, and databases. This process can be painful, temporarily disrupting productivity as everyone needs to learn a new system.

e. **New Strategic Direction.** One of the more exciting aspects of a business transition comes when new owners or management adopt an innovative marketing plan. Creating new products and entering new markets can bring the organization a fresh outlook and energy.

f. **Some Employees or Customers Depart.** One outcome can be that long-time employees loyal to the previous owners decide to leave. Mitigating this issue requires skill, tact, and understanding. Offering incentives may help the transition go smoother.

g. **Change in Vendors or Suppliers.** A company's new owners will often have their preferred suppliers and service providers, entities they have done business with before. For example, they may change the law firm the company uses to one they retained in the past.

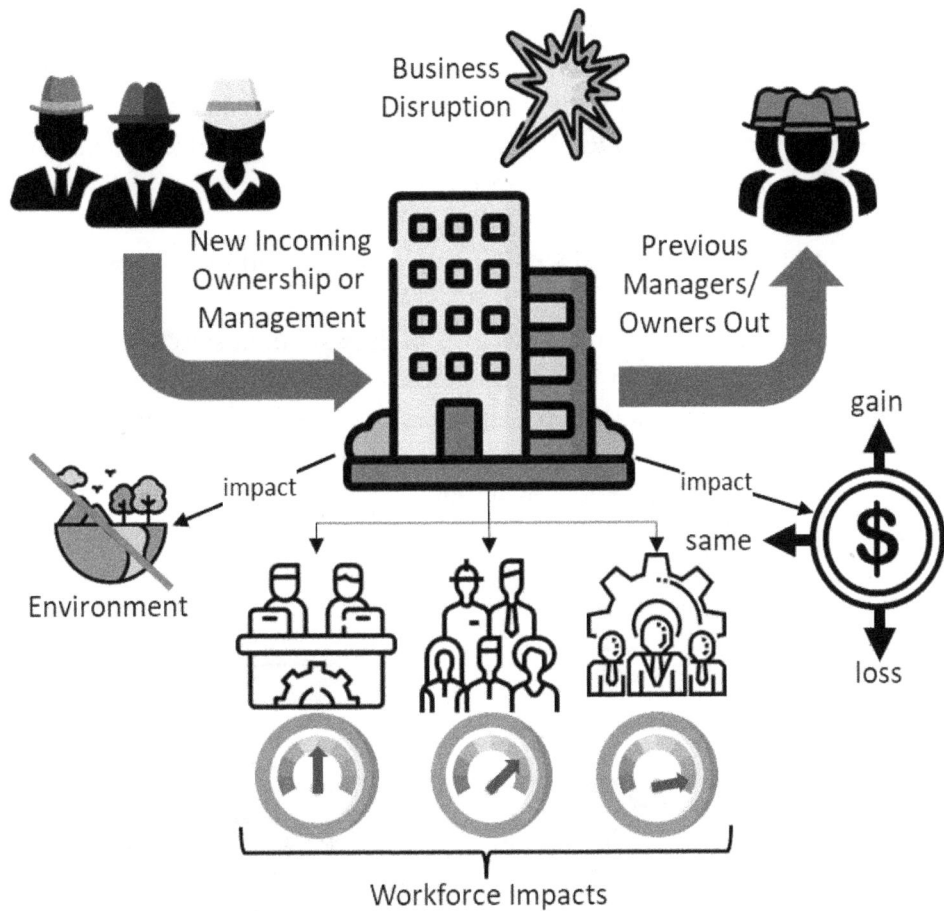

Figure 44: Graphic Depiction of Impacts when There Is Ownership Change Disruption

    h. **Community Relationships.** This topic is critical because of the organization's influence within the community. Maintaining a good relationship with the community and the public benefits all concerned. The workforce usually comes from the surrounding community, the business impacts the environment, and sponsorship and charity work are important for local relationships.

Solution. The solution to disruption planning can take several shapes. However, a few suggestions and recommendations can improve a company's Disruption Planning.

1. **Create a disruption plan.** This can be a chapter in an overall strategy or separate for this subject.
2. **Select a disruption team.** It is difficult and requires an alternate team because the selected personnel may cause ownership or managerial change.
3. **Involve your communications personnel and public relations staff.** Know what information can be shared and when it should be shared. Control the messages, handle transparency, and immediately nip rumors and false theories.
4. **Keep the strategy and specifics close hold.** This type of disruption moves quickly and sometimes requires real-time information and rapid decision-making. The rumor mill can go rampant and out of control. Thus, keep the information quiet until a strategy is settled and refer to the solution step #3 above.

5. **Create and conduct "what-if" scenarios.** Attempt to reflect on the type of sudden ownership change that can occur. This is an important step because it informs the leadership team that, at minimum, the subject has been discussed and considered.
6. **Finalize a strategy and schedule.** Ensure that the plan covers information flow to all stakeholders and considers their impact, reception, incentives, and integration into the new ownership.
7. **Tell key stakeholders upfront.** More surprises or being blind-sided complicates the process.
8. **Communicate clearly and openly.** This goes back to solution step #3. Transparency and truthfulness will go a long way in mitigating problems with the transition.
9. **Don't make promises you can't keep.** It seems obvious, but often, management gets caught in a trap and pledges the same resources to more than one entity. Figure 45 depicts the impacts of a change in ownership disruption.

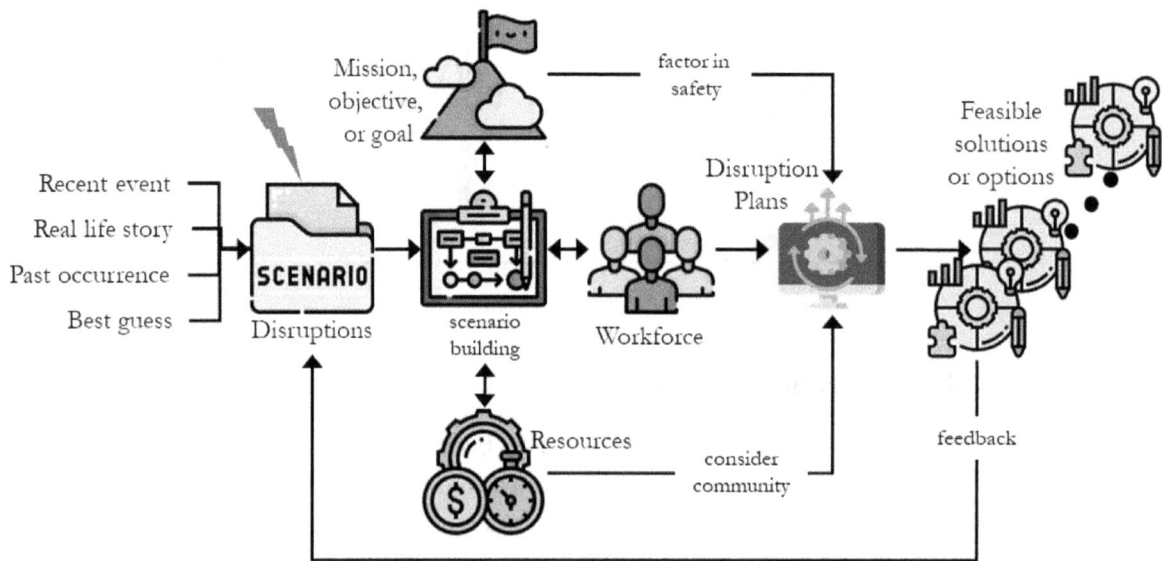

Figure 45: Starts with an Event & Proceeds to Feasible Solutions

Actions. When preparing for a sudden change in ownership, the most significant action is to prepare a Disruption Plan. The plan can have many items, as shown above in the solution section. Below are a few considerations that can be acted upon as needed. See Figure 46.

1. **Prepare for disruptions.** Entrepreneurs underestimate the stress and turmoil of an ownership change. The transition costs, adjusting to the new ownership culture, and unexpected expenses affect profitability. Create what-if scenarios to prepare for disruptions.
2. **Build in room for financing all phases of the transformation.** Abrupt ownership transitions are often highly leveraged, leaving little room to raise more money if forecasts are missed. Making matters worse, businesses usually use shorter-term loans to finance the transaction. Such loans come with lower interest rates but must be paid back quickly, squeezing cash flow in the critical aftermath of an ownership change.
3. **Consider an insider succession.** In a management or employee buyout, company insiders pool resources to acquire all or part of the business. It is often challenging to plan for this

64

during a disruption because of the suddenness and uncertainty of the nature of the many tragic events. Considerations for a successful insider transition:

a. **Be transparent.** Often, this appears to be noticeable but difficult to maintain. Events happen quickly, and getting the word out takes time. Good communication between the owner and managers is essential.

b. **Focus on the company's survival.** This includes the workforce, existing customers, suppliers, and the community. Cost cutting, improved productivity, or increased revenues may be needed.

c. **Select managers carefully.** The new ownership and senior management must have the right skills to take the company through the transition period and run the business profitably.

d. **Retain good relationships.** Establish reasonable incentives for everyone involved. Remember that the associations involve several entities, including the environment, the community, and the public. Disruption can influence the company to be a disruptee or a disruptor.

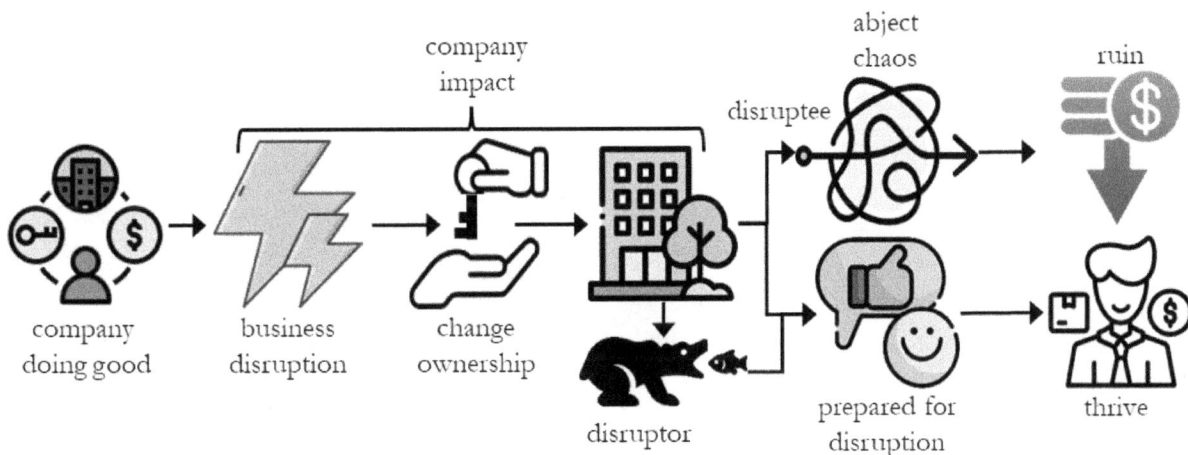

Figure 46: Ownership Change Results in a Disruptor or Disruptee

4. Don't count on intricate collaborations. A sudden, disruptive ownership change must often be conducted based on first impressions.

5. Cultivate dependable management. This is the key to a successful ownership transition. The new executives must have a good understanding of the business.

Summary. The most effective way to support organizational change is to develop processes that help achieve buy-in. When preparing a Disruption Plan, consider ways for all stakeholders to have some input into the process. Remember, scenario building needs to be accomplished upfront. Listen to the marketplace, the workforce, and the community. Good luck.

References & Bibliography.

1. Frost & Sullivan, "Unlock the full potential of your digital future," Avaya; 2020
2. Brian Hill, "What Happens When a Business Changes Hands," 2021
3. "What Legacy Endpoint Security Really Costs," CrowdStrike; January 15, 2022
4. "What is Change Management and How Does it Work," Prosci, People, Change, Results; 2021
5. Katie Taylor, "Change management steps that turn chaos into organized chaos," Work-Life; September 20, 2021
6. "Why business transitions often fail," BDC.ca; 2022
7. Chris Mercer, "10 Reasons That Businesses Change Ownership," CM Blog; 2021
8. Opportune LLP, "Organizational Change Management in The Age of Disruption," JDSupra; July 22, 2022
9. Brodie Woodland, "Managing Disruption During Organizational Change," Optimize Consulting; 2022
10. "Selling Your Business - A Guide for Entrepreneurs," bdc,ca; 2022

Category: Operations
Truth#12: Your supply chain will be disrupted.

Background & Introduction. Thanks to unforeseen supply insufficiencies, natural disasters, civil unrest, fuel shortages, and even traffic jams, supply chain disruptions are a fact of life. That's why shrewd organizations focus on being proactive. They prepare for disruption by creating business continuity plans, forming an immediate response team, and learning from past mistakes. The wise business leaders seek new knowledge and know-how to disrupt the marketplace, unsettling their competition. Subject matter experts suggest organizing the thought process:

Managing this complexity by structuring your thoughts into four categories.

1. **Strategic:** Ensures efficient product movement and communication.
2. **Tactical:** Determines transportation, production, scheduling, and research processes.
3. **Operational:** Determines the rate of production material, supply consumption, and flow of finished goods.
4. **Sustainment:** Considers failure, downtime, and long-term supply chain maintenance.

Much of the supply chain management disruption has recently involved changing the paradigm of how product purchasing power has been wielded. Instead of luring customers to the products by urging them to visit a store, the business now focuses on bringing the products to the customers. See Figure 47.

Figure 47: SCM Paradigm is Changing - Bring Products to the Customers

Supply chain management (SCM) often involves using supply chain software applications, which have virtually revolutionized the old manual systems. Today's SCM also utilizes Internet of Things (IoT) devices and communications to monitor and track the products from cradle to grave, providing real-time dashboards and decision assistance. SCM involves the flow of materials, finances, and information. This includes product design, planning, execution, monitoring, and control.

Purpose. This chapter suggests preparations that organizations can use to prepare for supply chain disruption. Both approaches are considered: Is your company the disruptor or the disruptee? The business leader who is ready for disruption is prepared when the unthinkable occurs and when their company launches a new product to shock the marketplace.

Challenge. The SCM process aims to reduce inventory, increase transaction speed, and improve workflow while focusing on profit. Software application tools and modules enhance and ensure SCM efficiency. Business leaders must be attentive to the marketplace horizon related to the supply chain. First, acquire a superb understanding of the company's supply chain. Second, real or virtual indicators should be placed at the chokepoints of the supply chain process. These will alert the disruption team when things are becoming uncertain. Third, create a disruption team that concentrates on innovative technology and can disrupt the supply chain. That is, it provides an advantage over the competition. That is the challenge for the business leader to be prepared for supply chain disruption.

Description. Supply chain disruption is not new but now has more impact. There are countless examples to learn from; note three listed below that impact consumer expectations caused by supply chain disruption. See Figure 48.

1991: When reports of poor working conditions at the Nike factories in Indonesia surfaced, Nike abdicated any responsibility for monitoring suppliers. As a result, Nike became the target of a global boycott that lasted years and profoundly impacted the demand for its products.

2014: After Disney's movie Frozen became a big hit, demand for toys based on the film far outstripped supply. Disney wrongly assumed toys based on Elsa and the gang wouldn't sell and failed to produce enough for Christmas. Parents took their protest to Twitter and Facebook.

2020: Amid the COVID-19 pandemic, two brothers bought 17,700 bottles of hand sanitizer. Amazon squashed its plans to sell on its platform at an exponentially marked-up price. To save face, the brothers donated the goods to first responders in Kentucky and Tennessee.

These examples emphasize the requirement for businesses to monitor all supply chain elements. This includes supplies, workers, distribution, customer service, and, most importantly, public relations. One more item: Stay attentive to feedback (all forms, e.g., social media) from all stakeholders.

Business Leaders should position their organizations to take advantage of innovative technology and supply chain ideas to become disruptors. See Figure 49. Many upcoming advancements are on the horizon that will change the very nature of delivering goods and services.

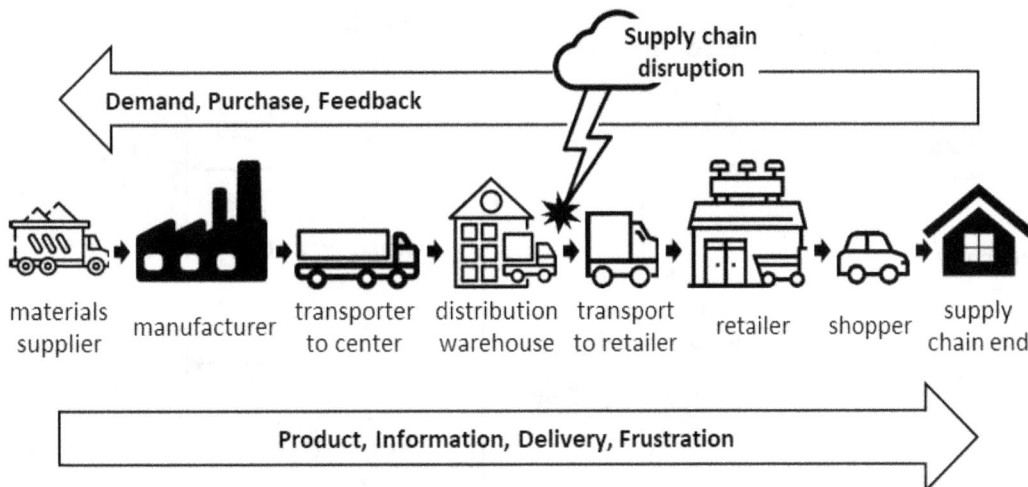

Figure 48: Illustration of how SCM Disruption Attacks Elements of the Supply Chain

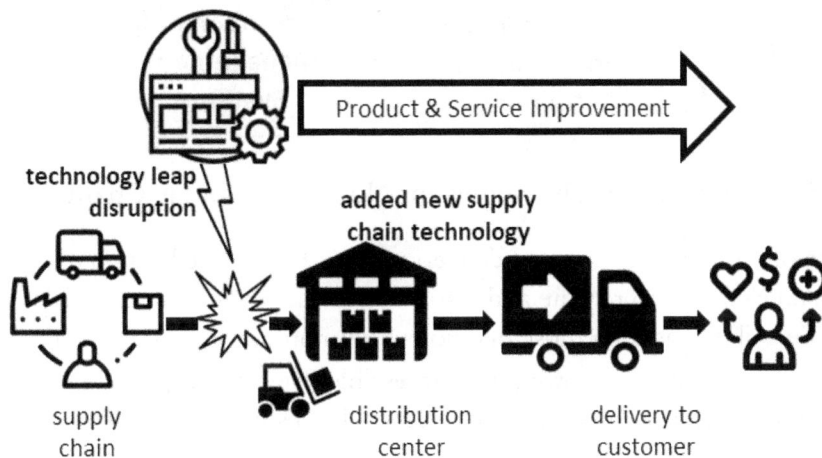

Figure 49: Disruption Opportunity Utilizing SCM Innovation

Solution. Adapting to change is challenging; the best preparation is practice. Develop "what if" scenarios the organization can discuss by hunting down resources, contacts, and alternate means of communicating your value proposition. A few thinking points are provided below to prepare for the impact of disruption and the opportunity to grow during an event. See Figure 50.

- Understand the impact of demand disruptions on the supply chain, the customer base, and the community. Resolve critical skills to meet near-term and future demand.
- Manage workforce safety and flexibility to maintain trust. Address their physical safety and mental well-being.
- Ensure the viability of the manufacturing ecosystem for each critical supply chain player, including material suppliers, contractor companies, co-manufacturers, logistics providers, and the community.

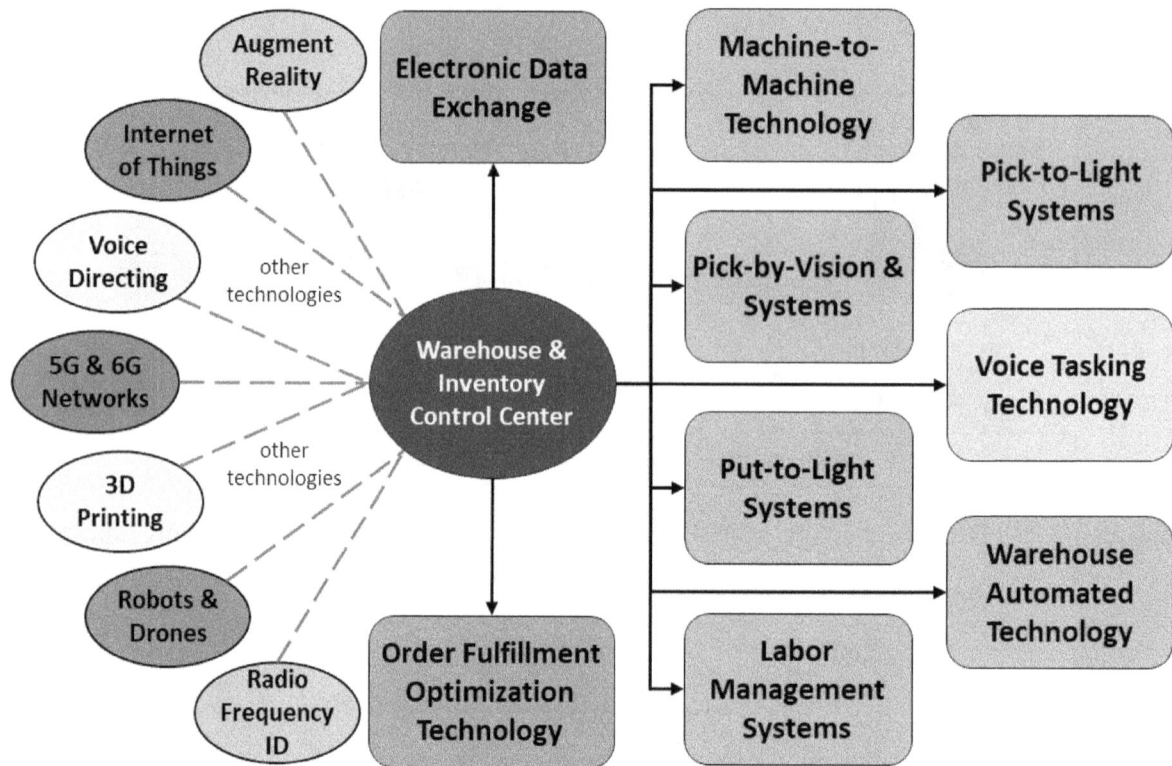

Figure 50: Innovative Technologies for No-Touch Supply Chain Disruption

- Rebalance physical production and delivery assets. Formulate backup plans to redeploy supply chain elements to reroute and resource critical production materials. Build greater resource flexibility, ensuring those decisions do not inhibit future growth.
- Leverage data capabilities, knowing that accessible data and advanced analytical capabilities respond more quickly, accurately, and successfully to supply chain disruptions.

In addition, Figure 51 provides six preparatory steps to improve disruption readiness.

1. **Prepare a Disruption Plan & Team.** Always start with demonstrating that people and resources are in place to respond, protect, and recover.
2. **Put People, Safety, & Security First.** Take care of the most important asset; that is how the organization strives and survives.
3. **Capture and leverage Data to Improve Visibility.** Data is the lifeblood of informed decision-making. It needs to be accurate, germane, and real-time.
4. **Segment Supply Chain to Prioritize Demand.** Break the supply chain into segments to explore alternatives ahead of time.
5. **Put Alert Sensors and IoT Devices Strategically in the Supply Chain.** These become a business's eyes and ears, ready to respond to red and green flags.
6. **Assess & Execute Supply Chain Scenarios.** Recommend - practice, practice, practice.

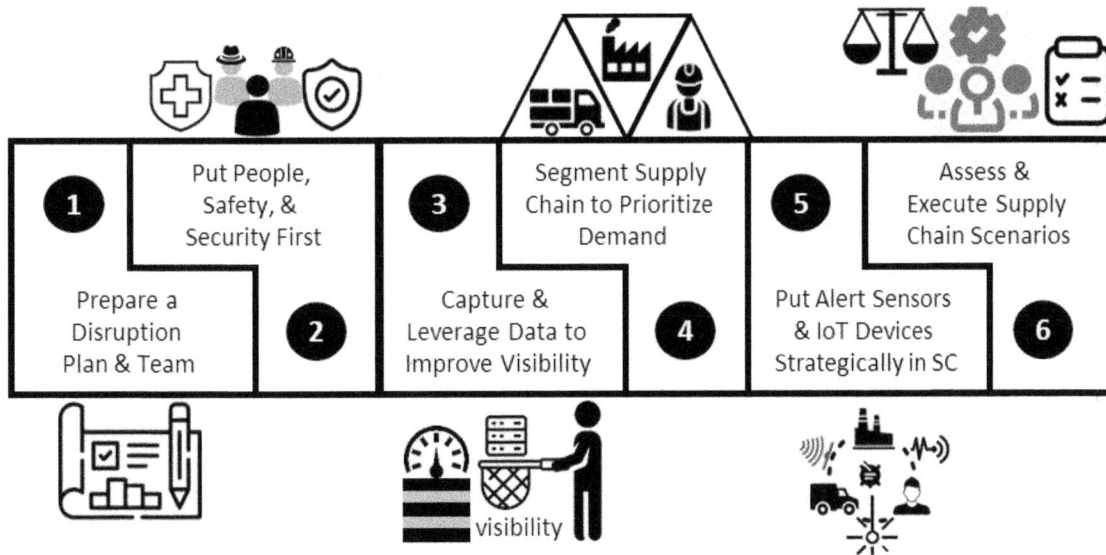

Figure 51: Six Preparation Suggestions for SCM Disruption

The diagram shows six numbered preparation suggestions:

1. Put People, Safety, & Security First
2. Prepare a Disruption Plan & Team
3. Segment Supply Chain to Prioritize Demand
4. Capture & Leverage Data to Improve Visibility
5. Assess & Execute Supply Chain Scenarios
6. Put Alert Sensors & IoT Devices Strategically in SC

Summary. Supply chain visibility (SCV) is at the forefront of business leaders' minds today. Businesses need to know where their product is, when it will be delivered, and every detail regarding the contents of the journey. It's also essential to provide this level of visibility to all the stakeholders in the supply chain. Plus, automate the process and take advantage of the new know-how. It can be overwhelming, so improve your readiness.

Is it any wonder we call this supply chain disruption? The skillset, wherewithal, and expertise required to deal with this magnitude of knowledge are daunting. For a business to be competitive, all this new technology gathers information to process and analyze to give decision-makers more feasible options. That enormity of data is intimidating. Consider placing a disruption menu on your dashboard to raise a red or green flag when a disruption opportunity presents itself.

References and Bibliography.

1. "Assessing the Total Cost of Supply Chain Damage," Spot See Brochure; July 1, 2018
2. "What's the Cost of Doing Nothing?" Separating Fact vs. Fiction in the Cloud netsuite.com; January 1, 2020
3. "Supply Chain Management (SCM) Explained," Technopedia; 2017
4. "Managing supply chains in times of uncertainty," HERE Technologies; 2020
5. "Supply chain disruption," Accenture; 2022
6. "Supply chain innovation: 4 challenges visibility can solve," HERE Technologies; 2020
7. Southam, Mark, "Disruption as a Business Strategy - How to Harness the Power of Disruption," www.certifyassoc.com, May 2020
8. Lofvers, Martijn, "No-nonsense," Supply Chain Movement, November 18, 2018; https://www.supplychainmovement.com/no-touch-nonsense/
9. "Warehouse Fulfillment – Move Material to the People, Not Vice Versa!", supplychaingamechanger.com, posted on March 16, 2020
10. "Supply chain visibility: 5 questions you're probably asking," Amazon Web Services (AWS) & HERE Technologies; 2021
11. "What's the Difference Between Fulfillment and Replenishment?," supplychaingamechanger.com, posted on February 19, 2020
12. "Supply Chain Management Tutorial," Simply Easy Learning; 2022
13. "Snafus in supply chain management," TechTarget.com; May 13, 2022

Category: Operations

Truth: #13. You will experience operational failure.

Background & Introduction. Operational disruption is defined as a business experience when unexpected events interrupt the smooth flow of operations in a shocking way.

Events whose impact is most significant are called "extreme events." They involve one or more of the following: the destruction of, or severe damage to, physical infrastructure and facilities; the loss or inaccessibility of personnel; and restricted access to the affected area. Five types of risk come to mind. See Figure 52.

Major operational disruptions can result from a wide range of events, such as earthquakes, hurricanes, weather-related events, terrorist attacks, and other

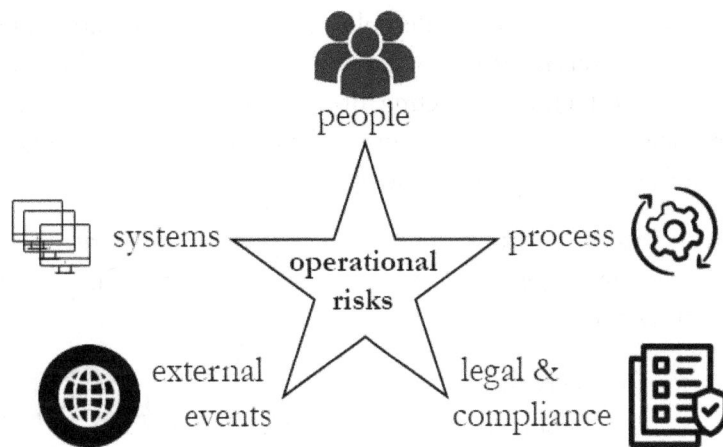

Figure 52: Operational Risks May Originate from Many Sources

intentional or accidental acts that cause widespread damage to the physical infrastructure. Other events, such as technology viruses, pandemics, and other biological incidents, may not cause widespread damage to the physical infrastructure but can nonetheless lead to significant operational disruptions by affecting the regular operation of the physical infrastructure in other ways.

With increased risk comes increased regulation and liability/accountability to the workforce, customer base, environment, and community. Disruption to operations (including supply chains) because of natural and man-made disasters is an unavoidable risk confronting each organization.

Purpose. This chapter focuses on operational failures severe enough to cause major disturbances in an organization's value chain, culture, and very existence. Companies need an understanding of their exposure, vulnerabilities, and potential losses to inform resilience strategies. See Equation 1.

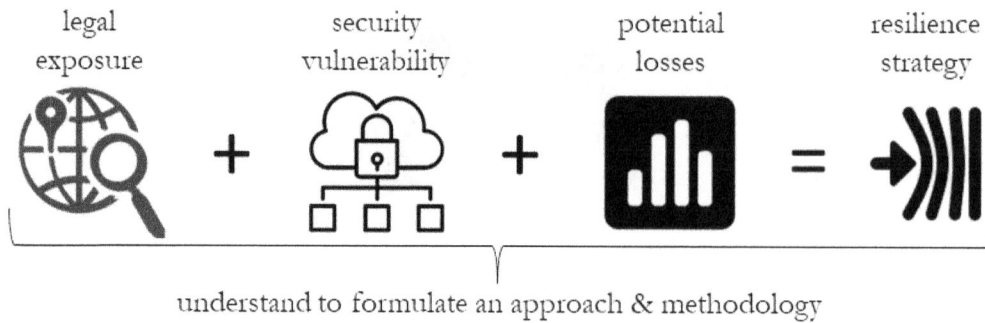

legal exposure + security vulnerability + potential losses = resilience strategy

understand to formulate an approach & methodology

Equation 1: Functions of Resilience

Challenge. Operational failures are an inevitable part of business life; therefore, focus on operational resilience and better disruption management. With shocks growing more frequent and severe, industry value chains vary in their level of disruption preparation.

The business value chain describes the full range of activities organizations perform to bring a product or service from conception to its end use and beyond. This includes activities such as design, production, marketing, distribution, and support to the consumer. An operational failure in any one of these areas can cause a disruption. The challenge is to provide tools, strategies, and suggestions to prepare for disruption because of an operational failure.

Description. Disruption when an organization experiences an operational failure may become a disaster. See Equation 2. Identifying and evaluating the impact of disasters on business provides the basis for the company to invest in:

- Recovery plans
- Prevention strategies
- Mitigation responses
- Scenario visualization

recovery + prevention + mitigation + scenarios = prepared

Equation 2: Disruption Preparation Formula

A disaster is an event whose timing is unexpected and whose consequences are seriously destructive. See Table 4 for a list of disasters that can impact business operations and cause failures with a big wallop. Any of these disruptions or a hybrid of more than one impacts business operations in the workplace and affects the workforce. Upon occurrence, they will require an immediate response. These events are characterized by four elements: (1) Suddenness, (2) Unexpectedness, (3) Significant destruction and/or loss of life, and (4) Lack of foresight or planning.

Man-Made Disasters	Natural Disasters
IT Threats	Weather-Related Threats
• Anonymous Cyber Threats	• Winter Storms
• Hackers	• Tornadoes
• Network design, equipment, operation	• Volcanoes

Terrorist Threats	• Earthquakes
• September 11, 2001 Terrorist Attacks	• Hurricanes, typhoons, cyclones
• 2010 Time Square Car Bombing	• Floods
• 2011 Norway Bombings	• Lightening, hail
• 2013 Boston Marathon	Pandemics
Civil Disturbances	• Avian Flu
• Anonymous Protests	• Swine Flu
• Occupy Wall Street Campaign	• MERS
Insider Threats	• Ebola
• Internal Sabotage	• Covid-19
• Workplace Violence/Active Shooter	Environment
• Power grid, hazardous material, safety	• Climate change, ozone layer

Table 4: Examples of Man-Made & Natural Disasters that Result in Disruption

Case Study Example: "Anonymous Cyber Attack"

Situation. In the early days of radio frequency identification applications, it was a very competitive environment.

We were so busy rushing our projects to market that we failed to think through everything that could go wrong. Any demo opportunity was often taken without regard for the environment or the audience.

Product. Our product placed sensors connected to a radio frequency transmitter inside a high-value asset container. The sensors monitored the relative humidity and temperature inside the container. Broadcast on an FCC-approved frequency, the conditions inside the container could be monitored periodically to prevent moisture accumulation and, eventually, water inside the container.

Competition. In one demo, we used an actual container with our device attached and "cast" the readings onto a theater screen. All our competitors and potential customers were present.

Several competing devices used the same frequency, but everything worked perfectly when we tested the system several times the night before.

Results. Our presentation highlighted the project's ability to protect high-value assets such as aircraft engines and avionics that are frequently transported in containers and metal and plastic. Our discriminator was the size of the device. Small enough to fit through the container site glass, the Integrated Sensor and Radio Frequency Identification Device (ISRFID) required no container modification other than removing the site glass and inserting the ISRFID device.

Challenge. A few minutes into the presentation, we discovered that the device was not communicating with our handheld computer and, therefore, not casting to the theater screen. With no other recourse, we continued with the PowerPoint presentation.

A question from the audience suggested a possible reason for the failure. One of our competitors asked if we had tested the device for interference in an RF noisy environment. Of course, we had, but this competitor seemed to know more about this environment than we did.

Suggestions. Many possible scenarios, like this case study, may be considered. The disruption team should frame improbable (shocking) scenarios, ascertain possible failures, assess disruption risks, and prepare for an occurrence. Examples of disruption scenarios are listed below:

Physical damage to a building

1. Damage to or breakdown of machinery, systems, or equipment
2. Severe ecosystem events (e.g., hurricanes, earthquakes, and/or forest fires)
3. Restricted access to a site or building
4. Interruption of the supply chain, including a supplier's failure or disruption of transportation of goods from the supplier.
5. Utility outage (e.g., electrical power outage)
6. Health pandemic or hazardous environment
7. Societal protest (e.g., religious, crime, ethnic, terrorist)
8. Damage to, loss, or corruption of information technology, including voice and data communications, servers, computers, operating systems, applications, and data
9. Absenteeism of essential employees (e.g., security breach, labor action, safety issues, protection equipment)

Recognize that operational failures are an inevitable part of business life. Therefore, the focus should be on operational resilience and better management of such incidents.

Solution. An organization can take action to prepare for disruption. Assign the task to an able leader and a team with varied skill sets, one of which is good at storyboarding.

Conduct a business impact analysis (BIA) for the disruption plan. It predicts the consequences of business function disruption or process and will gather information needed to develop recovery strategies.

Potential loss scenarios should be identified during a risk assessment. Operations may also be interrupted by the failure of a supplier of goods or services or delayed deliveries. There are many possible scenarios that should be considered.

Conduct a business operations impact analysis as part of practicing with your team utilizing scenarios. Consider the following steps when performing the risk assessment for each scenario. See Figure 53.

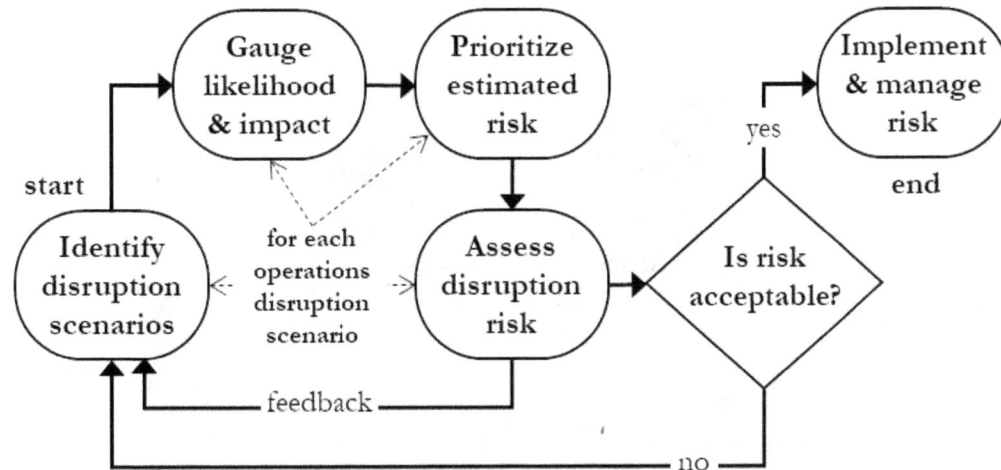

Figure 53: Risk Assessment Process for Each Scenario

The impact analysis should identify the operational and financial impacts of disrupting business functions and processes. This is all part of the scenario process. Impacts to consider include:

- Lost sales and income
- Delayed sales or income
- Increased expenses (e.g., overtime labor, outsourcing, expediting costs, etc.)
- Regulatory fines
- Contractual penalties or loss of contractual bonuses
- Customer dissatisfaction or defection
- Delay of new business plans
- Employee and customer safety
- Cyber-attack outcomes

Another consideration is the timing and duration of the disruption. The point in time when a business function or process is disrupted can significantly affect the loss sustained. The duration of the disruption could be measured in seconds, days, months, and/or years.

Experiencing operational failure will, by definition, create downtime. Downtime can result in disrupted business processes, lower productivity, and reduced cycle times and activity rates. It also can cause employees to become frustrated with their inability to access key applications and data.

However, employees are not the only ones affected by downtime; unfortunately, in today's web-enabled businesses, customers are affected too. During downtime, organizations can lose customers who go to other vendors or providers. The resulting diminished market reputation can also lead to reduced business from remaining customers. In short, over time, downtime and system-related issues can hurt profits because of higher operating expenses and lower revenue.

Bring in public relations at the first sign of disruption. One of the most important aspects of surviving post-disruption is how the public, customers, government, and the industry perceive your performance. See Figure 54.

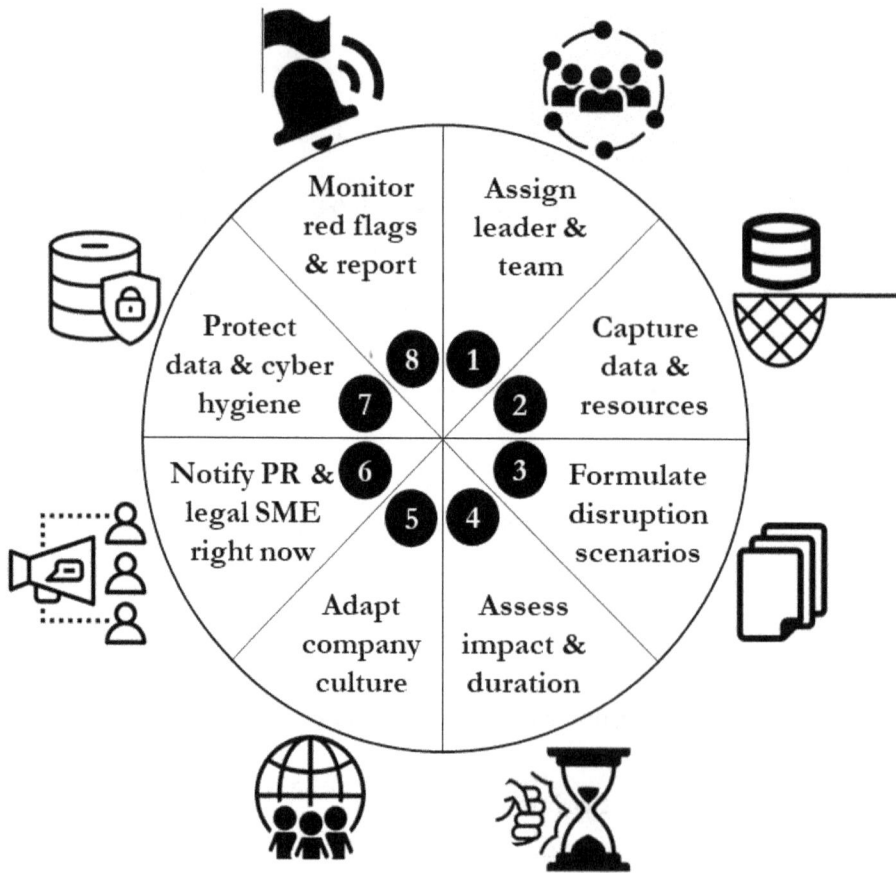

Figure 54: Disruption Plan for Experiencing Operational Failure

Risk mitigation may face a more daunting challenge, and it is internal. The organizational culture must foster an adaptable climate for change to evolve during disruption. This is another facet of preparing for disruption when you experience operational failure.

Summary. Companies are now suffering from a wide variance of operational failure rates. These failures feed into operating income loss. However, the means to identify and manage the risks of these losses exist. Those firms at risk need to know, measure, and mitigate it. The business must look carefully at its operations to find new efficiencies, apply new technologies, and implement new improvement approaches. It must also identify from a holistic perspective where vulnerabilities reside and implement programs to manage them. The results will pay continuing dividends to the organization.

References & Bibliography.

1. Dominic Essuman, "Operational resilience, disruption, and efficiency: Conceptual and empirical analyses," Elsevier; November 15, 2020
2. Raymond Boggs, "Business Operations Disruption Risk: Identify, Measure, Reduce," IDC Analyze the Future; December 15, 2009
3. Neil Hodge, "Dealing with Disruption," Risk Management Magazine; October 1, 2019
4. Mike Cowan, "Operational failures are inevitable — manage them!" Thomson Reuters Institute; June 17, 2022
5. M.Todinov, "Probabilistic Risk Assessment & Risk Management," ScienceDirect Topics; 2017
6. "Business Impact Analysis," Ready.gov; 2022
7. Susan Lund, "Risk, resilience, and rebalancing in global value chains," McKinsey; August 6, 2020

Category: Operations
Truth #14. You will receive bad publicity.

Background & Introduction. Any organization leader should exercise disruption awareness often. Armed with a disruption plan, the leader confronts the disruption head-on with the disruption team. They perform measured actions designed to mitigate the effects of the disruption and create an opportunity to succeed.

Bad publicity impacts your business operations daily in all phases. Every company should be prepared for the inevitable bad publicity crisis, such as a data breach, executive scandal, workplace harassment, failed events, or corporate impropriety. An increasing number of businesses value the importance of a crisis management plan for disruption. The impact is felt across several business operations at once. A bad publicity disruption hits an organization, creating near-term and long-term problems. We aren't talking about bad customer reviews, one or two disgruntled employees, or not picking up the trash. Bad publicity disruption potentially creates a disaster. Your company will struggle to walk away unscathed. Examples are mishandling hazardous waste, workplace harassment, corporate fraud, etc. Recently, this seems to occur more often and with a more significant impact. See Figure 55.

Figure 55: Bad Publicity Creates Disruption

Environmental change, armed conflicts, bad publicity, and government actions may strike a business right in its core all at once. At first blush, the business leader says what can I do to get ready for fate, bad luck, an act of God, or the act of a madman? The fighter says, "We can do plenty to be prepared!" The survivor has a crisis management plan, calling it a disruption strategy, and is ready to execute it to meet challenges immediately and even turn a threatening set of events into a prospect. There are several things that an organization can do to prepare for bad publicity disruption.

Purpose. This chapter examines approaches for an organizational leader or governance board to reach a reasonable and affordable readiness posture to elevate their preparedness for business disturbance caused by bad publicity. The main objective is to provide the leader with a framework to prepare for disruption.

Challenge. The high costs of natural catastrophes, acts of terrorism, severe weather, and other disasters that can directly affect businesses are well known. As organizations react in the interest of their employees, suppliers, and customers, they can trigger a piggyback disruption, such as bad publicity. That is, poor crisis management leads to more disruption.

In the last decade alone, significant disruptions have resulted from:

- Political and social unrest.
- Bad publicity due to product failure, workplace harassment, & corporate impropriety.
- Cyber-attacks and technology failures.
- Pandemics and epidemics.
- Supply chain interruptions, including supplier bankruptcies.
- Port closures due to labor strikes.
- Loss of business stemming from terrorist attacks and mass shootings.
- Regulatory actions from local, state, & federal governments.
- Raw materials shortages.
- Product recalls or contamination events.

Solution. Adapting to change can be a big challenge for many businesses. However, as disruptive transformations turn many industries upside down, adaptability is increasingly essential for entrepreneurs. Change is the only constant in the business world.

We don't overcome disruption by being stronger or more intelligent than our competitors but by being better able to adapt to it. The steps below are things a business can do (using the CERTIFY process) to prepare for disruption caused by bad publicity. The first step is to create a disruption plan to prevent and mitigate bad publicity. See the checklist below and Figure 56 for a straightforward approach to an organization's disruption plan.

1. Identify risks & prioritize by disturbance value.
2. Assign roles & responsibilities to the crisis team.
3. Recognize triggers to activate the disruption plan.
4. Establish & agree on a spokesperson for the public & stakeholders.
5. Determine the most strategic locations for the team and supplies & formulate responses.
6. Document plans, record actions, conduct an exercise, & discuss lessons learned.

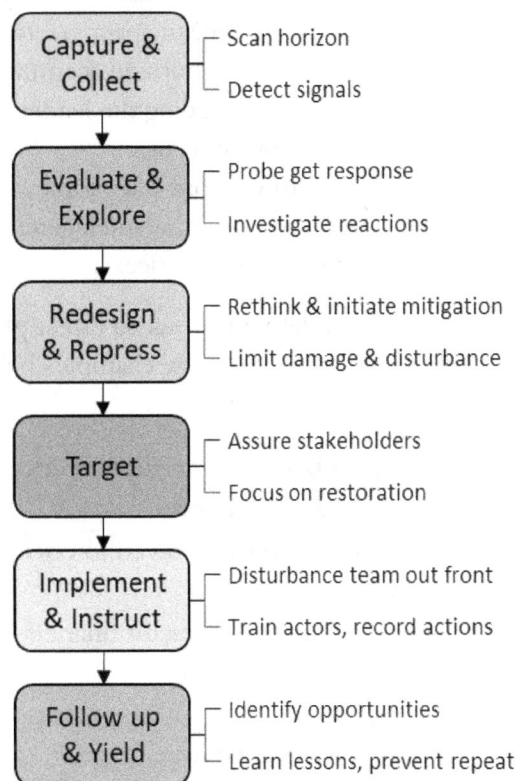

Capture & Collect
- Scan horizon
- Detect signals

Evaluate & Explore
- Probe get response
- Investigate reactions

Redesign & Repress
- Rethink & initiate mitigation
- Limit damage & disturbance

Target
- Assure stakeholders
- Focus on restoration

Implement & Instruct
- Disturbance team out front
- Train actors, record actions

Follow up & Yield
- Identify opportunities
- Learn lessons, prevent repeat

Figure 56: Disruption Plan Approach

Description. Businesses must navigate the financial and operational challenges of disruption while rapidly addressing the needs of their people, customers, and suppliers. Organizational leaders can turn massive complexity and business disturbance into meaningful change by taking the right actions.

An organization receiving negative, humiliating, or damaging publicity may face disaster. PR crises are serious. The popularity of social media means that a crisis can be spread globally instantly. Trying to stop a crisis from going viral online is virtually impossible. Businesses must respond to the immediate impacts of one disruption, perhaps followed by another, and prepare for what comes next. These actions will help to optimize results and mitigate risks.

Actions. There are many directions that a business can embark upon when trying to improve disruption readiness. It is important to remember that these are unpredictable situations that arise. Thus, the best thing that can be done is to

1. Get prepared ahead of time by producing a disruption plan.
2. Assign disruption roles to your team.
3. Run scenarios through a series of storyboard-like exercises.
4. Maintain cyber hygiene, inspect safety features, and safeguard emergency supplies.
5. Remain vigilant using horizon scanning.
6. Train employees, including the leadership structure.
7. Consider insurance coverage.
8. Prepare a hotlist of front-page topics from the environment, politics, culture, arts, law enforcement, and business intelligence and review it each morning. Please keep it to five bullet points or less. Practice.

Most businesses are set up to react to direct physical damage but consider options that address many other disruption types. See a few examples below. Any one of these disruptions can also generate bad publicity.

- Contingent business interruption coverage, which can protect against physical damage suffered by key suppliers.
- Cyber protection has evolved to cover not just data breaches but technology-driven business interruption.
- Political risk and trade credit financing can cover exposures related to government actions, instability, and insolvency.
- Non-damage business interruption policies (NDBI) can provide coverage for revenue loss without a physical damage trigger.

The next step is to measure your public relations. There are several tools on the market to assist in this. One is your ESG (Environmental, Social, & Governance) score, and the other is SEO, which stands for Search Engine Optimization. A third instrument may be to use AVE (Advertising value equivalency). These are ways for public relations and communications agencies to measure the impact of media coverage. Finally, horizon scanning systematically examines information to identify potential threats, risks, emerging issues, and opportunities for your organization. All of these can aid in disruption preparedness. Figure 57 provides a step-by-step method for articulating your action plan. Other actions include:

- Stop the crisis before it ever happens.
- Stay ahead of the story to buy valuable time and stay in control.
- Focus on actions before you focus on words.
- Express proper sympathies and then make sure they get heard by those who matter.
- Stress the information you can share.
- Do a proper post-mortem to grow your standing and stop it from happening again.

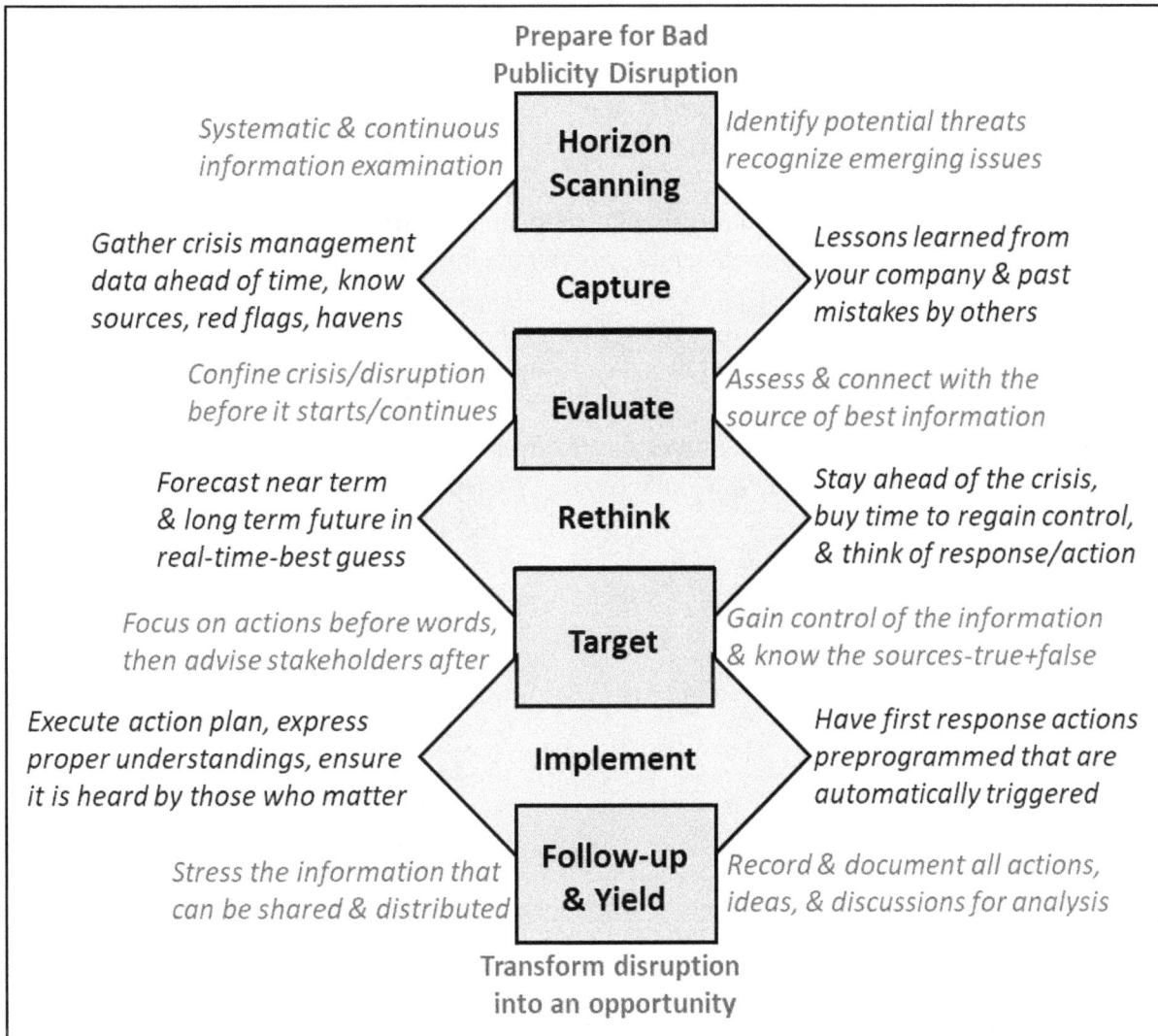

Prepare for Bad
Publicity Disruption

Horizon Scanning

Systematic & continuous information examination

Identify potential threats recognize emerging issues

Capture

Gather crisis management data ahead of time, know sources, red flags, havens

Lessons learned from your company & past mistakes by others

Evaluate

Confine crisis/disruption before it starts/continues

Assess & connect with the source of best information

Rethink

Forecast near term & long term future in real-time-best guess

Stay ahead of the crisis, buy time to regain control, & think of response/action

Target

Focus on actions before words, then advise stakeholders after

Gain control of the information & know the sources-true+false

Implement

Execute action plan, express proper understandings, ensure it is heard by those who matter

Have first response actions preprogrammed that are automatically triggered

Follow-up & Yield

Stress the information that can be shared & distributed

Record & document all actions, ideas, & discussions for analysis

Transform disruption
into an opportunity

Figure 57: Step-by-Step Action Plan using CERTIFY Methodology

Summary. A disruption (by definition) will be a surprise. But your plan of attack should already be prepared. Your organization will be judged on how it responds. You'll need a disruption plan and a disruption response team. You'll need trained personnel and social media monitoring. You'll need damage limitation to protect the reputation of your company.

References and Bibliography.

1. McCoy, Julie, "10 Ways to Avoid Bad Press," Search Engine Journal; June 13, 2020
2. Candice Landau "How to Handle and Avoid Negative Publicity," BPlans; 2021
3. "7 Tips for Surviving Through a Bad Publicity Storm ," Grand Marketing Solutions; 2019
4. "How To Deal With Negative Press In A Positive Way," Forbes Agency Council; 2/28/2019
5. "What are the effects of reputational damage?," The Business Continuity Institute; September 27, 2017
6. Charlotte Rogers, "How Brands Can Bounce Back from Disaster," Marketing Week Knowledge Center; April 24, 2017
7. "PR Crisis eBook; It's not IF it happens. It's WHEN." Talkwalker; 2022
8. "13 Ways for Companies to Successfully Recover from Bad Press," Forbes Coaches Council; June 25, 2021
9. Mathew Donald, "How Can You Measure Disruption?" Venture Magazine; April 2, 2021
10. Nicole Salimbeni, "Avoid disruption and focus on core business," PriceWaterhouseCoopers; 2019
11. Soren Kaplan, "Disrupt or be disrupted," PriceWaterhouseCoopers; October 15, 2016
12. Ashish Sarkar & Christoph Zinke, "Decoding disruption," KPMG; October 18, 2017
13. "Why you have been measuring PR impact wrong," Signal AI; 2021
14. "How to prepare for and manage a PR crisis effectively," Signal AI; 2021
15. Anna Grabtchak, "How to Do Horizon Scanning_ A Step-by-Step Guide," Futures Platform; October 5, 2021

Category: Operations

Truth #15. Business processes will break down.

Background & Introduction. Everyone talks about business processes, but it is essential to understand what they are, what they do for your business, and, more importantly, what occurs when they are disrupted. A business process is a series of steps a group of workers performs to achieve a concrete goal or objective. A business process, business method, or business function is a collection of related, structured activities or tasks that produce a service or product by people or equipment of a particular customer. Figure 58 provides many areas where companies rely on business processes to get work done efficiently, on time, within budget, and is repeatable.

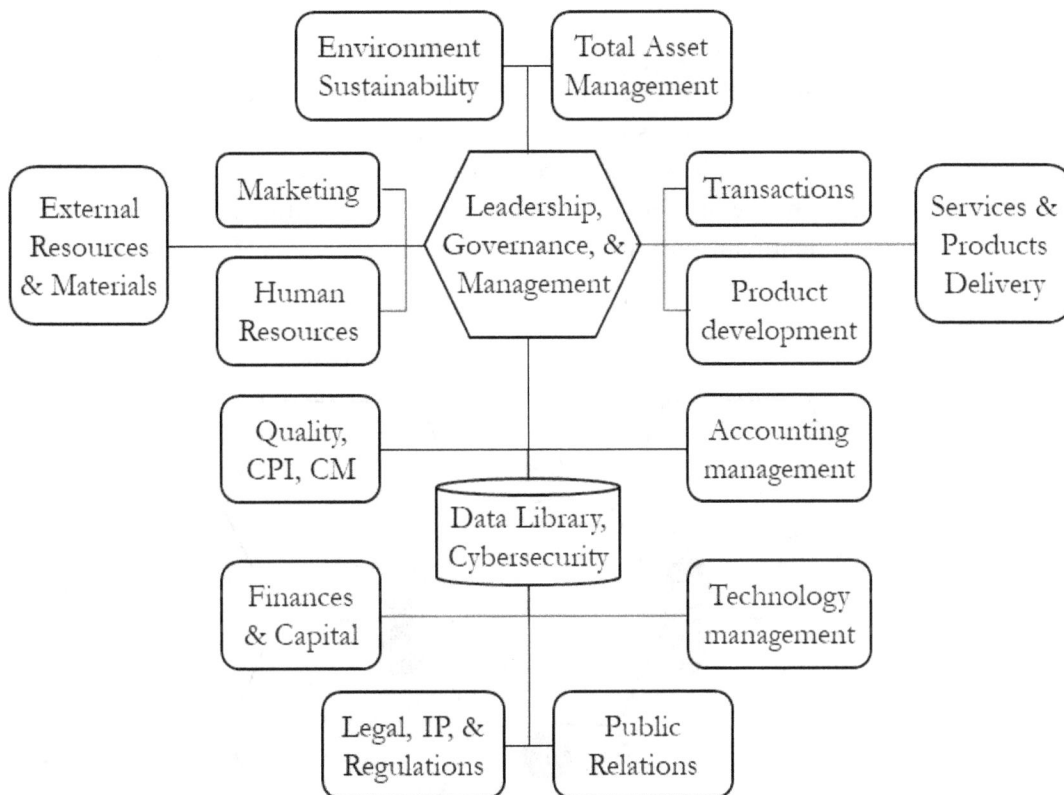

Figure 58: Examples of Organizational Departments Using Business Processes

It is quickly apparent that any disruption in one or more of the business areas shown in Figure 1 will cause severe problems in others and throughout the organization. A process forms a lifeline for any business and helps it streamline individual activities, ensuring that resources are optimized. Four essential attributes constitute an ideal business process:

1. **Established and Finite** – A good business process has well-defined starting and ending points and a finite number of steps.
2. **Replicable & Repeatable** – A good business process runs an indefinite number of times.
3. **Creates value** – It aims to translate value creation into executable tasks and produce meaningful results.
4. **Adaptable and Flexible** – It has an inherent nature to be flexible to change and is not rigid. This is a continuous characteristic of business processes; they must be susceptible to improvement and transform smoothly as needed.

Importantly, for this paper, business processes must sound an alert when they sense a disturbance and be prepared to react quickly during a disruption.

Purpose. Business process transformation means radically changing a series of actions needed to meet a specific business goal. This approach ensures that a company's employees, goals, processes, and technologies are all prepared to respond when disruption occurs. This chapter aims to discuss this critical concept, examine a couple of examples, and provide a set of actions that a business can utilize to become prepared for business process disruption and minimize its effects in a timely manner. See Figure 59.

Challenges. At a fundamental level, the process specifies how things are accomplished in an organization. On the other hand, the very definition of disruption is a disturbance or problem with the process. This difference is essential, as no process is perfect or sacred. Organizations that succeed during a disruption are not those who have the exact right processes in place but those who can recognize and adjust as change happens. New opportunities presented themselves, or problems resulted. The challenge is identifying and reacting to the first heads-up and/or warning.

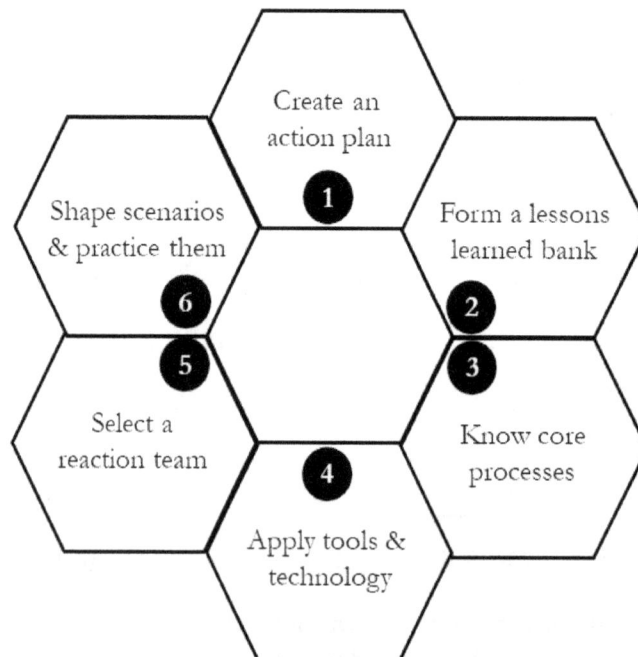

Figure 59: Preparing for Business Process Disruption

Solution. The organization's response to disruption can range from complete chaos to creating a golden prospect to strengthen the business. Disruption preparedness for a company to be agile, foreknowing, and flexible to a process disturbance is simple and complicated. The following considerations are presented to establish a foundation.

1. **Create an action plan.** It is not necessarily a formal document but has a course of action that alerts the management of an upcoming change, automatically begins gathering data, and launches a reaction team.

2. **Form a repository of lessons learned.** Examples include other situations involving the company's processes. Perhaps the company has undergone a digital transformation, dealt with an environmental problem, and/or experienced a legal challenge to the company's core processes. These previous experiences go a long way in forming a business process disruption response. Capture and replicate process changes so the organization can build success over time.

3. **Know the company's processes.** Management must be familiar with how work is completed within the organization. They should have a fundamental understanding that makes them more comfortable with rapidly evolving the business apparatus and processes as needed. Process knowledge and iteration wisdom become institutional.

4. **Apply tools, software, and other technology.** These instruments enable the organization to add scale, efficiency, accuracy, and acceleration to the process transformation, mitigation, and prospect promotion.

5. **Select a reaction team.** The group should consist of subject matter experts who act as first responders to quickly assess what is happening, evaluate alternatives, rethink processes, and target possible options.

6. **Fashion scenarios and practice.** Use existing or uniquely generated happenings germane to the organization and business climate. Storyboard the situation and possible response, including the public relations spin and its effect on the employees—document findings to compare over time.

Description. Organizations implement business process management strategies to improve company operations to simplify workflows, boost productivity, reduce compliance risks, eliminate waste, lower costs, enrich customer experiences, and increase agility, scalability, and process efficiency. Figure 60 provides a process flow chart showing a disruption during the transition between steps 2 and 3.

The process flow provides a path to begin a management response immediately, highlights initial steps to gather information, assess the situation, and rethink or redesign the process. Options exist to try again or abandon altogether and start anew. Note that there are specific points to provide feedback information or to modify process actions to meet the requirements for mitigation and return to service.

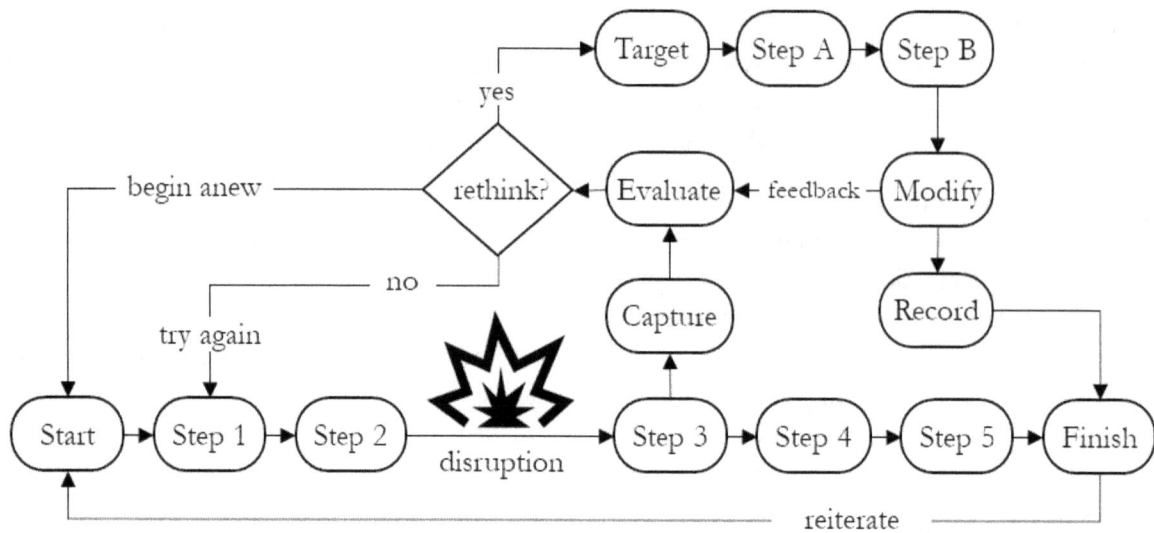

Figure 60: Simplified Process Disruption Flow Chart

Summary. Well-designed business processes set an organization on the path to success. Everyone is clear on their roles and responsibilities and works with a clear vision of the end goal. Disruption is unfortunate but inevitable, and the enterprise is well-served when prepared for these disturbances.

This chapter discusses a business process disruption approach and strategy to prepare your business. As the chapter title states, Business Processes will Break down.

References & Bibliography.

1. Mary Ann Anderson, "How to Manage Process Disruptions in Operations Management," Dummies a Wiley Brand; April 10, 2017
2. Clayton Christensen. "Business Disruptions Explained," Strategy for Executives; 2022
3. Gustavo Gomez, "What Disruption Teaches Us About Process," Forbes; July 10, 2020
4. George Lawton, "7 business process management challenges and how to fix them," Tech Target; April 27, 2022
5. "5 Business Disruption Examples and Key Takeaways," SpriggHR; July 14, 2020
6. "Business Process - Definition, Lifecycle Steps, and Importance," KissFlow; April 19, 2022

Category: Customer

Truth #16. Consumers' tastes and expectations will change.

Background & Introduction. All businesses and workplaces experience change, but some changes are more impactful than others. Sometimes, significant cultural or technological events can completely change the market. Known as disruptive change, these large shifts in consumer behavior and expectations influence how businesses develop and market their products and services.

Disruptive change requires high-level strategic responses from company leadership to ensure the company's long-term survival. When disruptive change occurs, current products and services may lose value. Disruptive change shapes how businesses interact with customers and their organizations. See Figure 61.

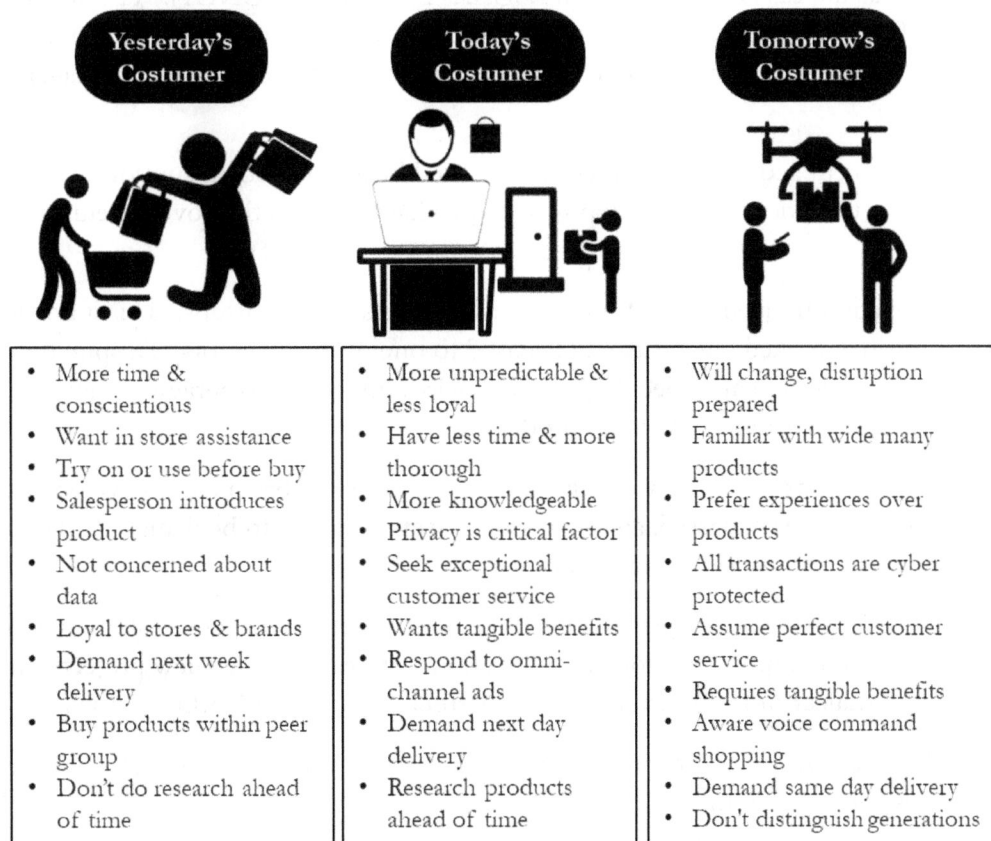

Yesterday's Costumer	Today's Costumer	Tomorrow's Costumer
• More time & conscientious • Want in store assistance • Try on or use before buy • Salesperson introduces product • Not concerned about data • Loyal to stores & brands • Demand next week delivery • Buy products within peer group • Don't do research ahead of time	• More unpredictable & less loyal • Have less time & more thorough • More knowledgeable • Privacy is critical factor • Seek exceptional customer service • Wants tangible benefits • Respond to omni-channel ads • Demand next day delivery • Research products ahead of time	• Will change, disruption prepared • Familiar with wide many products • Prefer experiences over products • All transactions are cyber protected • Assume perfect customer service • Requires tangible benefits • Aware voice command shopping • Demand same day delivery • Don't distinguish generations

Figure 61: Examples of Customer Notions

Business owners must adapt to disruption to prevent their businesses from failing and becoming unable to compete with new consumer behavior and expectations.

Purpose. This chapter examines why consumer behavior and expectations can trigger disruption in an organization or industry. It provides clear action items that business leadership can adopt in advance to prepare their company, workforce, and stakeholders for disruption.

Challenge. Consumers' tastes and expectations will change, and consumer beliefs and behaviors are rapidly transforming. Businesses must leverage deep consumer insights to keep up with the pace and maybe even stimulate those changes.

A disruptor's competitive advantage comes from product innovation and the ability to modify consumer behavior. A true disruption, therefore, does more than affect purchasing patterns; it changes purchasing behavior within the market or industry. This is the challenge: Utilize behavior science to recognize customer sensitivities and prepare for disruption.

Case Study Example: "Consumer tastes will change"

Event. Government customers frequently change jobs. Often, the government customer who worked with you to develop an innovative project moves to another job before completion.

Situation. Such was the case for the patented Logistics Network (LOGNET). The network connected radio frequency identification devices (RFID) on an FCC-approved frequency. This enabled RFID devices to connect from a remote asset via an ad hoc network to a management information system.

Funded by a government acquisition command and tested in an operational environment, the project was ready to transition from development to production when the government project lead transferred.

Challenge. Innovation frequently comes from small businesses and startups. This innovation was developed at a top-five-ranked university and licensed to one of the inventors. Despite these credentials, the new government project lead needed help convincing his superiors that the innovation team could transition to full-rate production.

Instead, the government project lead was directed to use an existing provider to develop an alternative. Two decades have passed, and high-value assets continue to be damaged. The government still needs an alternative innovation.

Comment. Risk-averse customers, particularly in the government, reduce the risk of $400 hammers but occasionally miss the opportunity for real innovation. It's easier to sell new projects on the reputation of the producer or manufacturer if your partner is Lockheed Martin or Boeing.

However, big defense companies are rarely interested in low-volume sales, even when they offer high-value returns for the customer.

Result. So, it was with LOGNET. Despite requests to team or sublicense with the government's chosen prominent defense business provider, the project died when the startup ran out of money.

Description. Disruption can impact a company in critical areas such as finances, products and services, operations, and relationships. It affects pricing, cost of goods, merchandized offerings, and manufacturing processes, including equipment, labor, supply chain, IoT networks, and communications. It also transforms the organizations' rapport with the community, government, and stakeholders. Business leadership may want to brush up on behavioral science to participate in the future marketplace driven by consumer expectations and performance.

Behavioral science is defined as various disciplines dealing with human actions, usually including sociology, psychology, and behavioral aspects of biology, economics, geography, law, psychiatry, and political science.

Understanding customer sensibilities is essential. Some topics for study are provided below to identify with customers, the workforce, and the community. Signals can, when monitored, give a pattern of disturbance, allowing the organization to predict a disruption. See Figure 62.

Indicators of disruptive change in consumer behavior	off	on
Government & industry regulations or rules changes	○	●
Limited supply chain availability or delivery malfunction	○	●
Lower volume of customer interactions & engagements	●	○
Decreased customer satisfaction & expectations	●	○
Specialties entering the mainstream marketplace	●	○
Changing public opinion & culture transformation	○	●
Technology advances that change the landscape	○	●
New or different competitors entering the industry	●	○
One or more 'on' signals may forecast a disruption coming	off	on

Figure 62: Indicators of Disruptive Consumer Behavior

1. **Reinforce positive new beliefs.** According to behavioral science, a consumer's set of beliefs about the world is a key influencer of consumer behavior. Figuring out what is important to consumers is crucial to understanding their behavior.

2. **Shape emerging habits with new products.** Companies can nudge consumers toward new habits through product innovation. For example, the recent pandemic has spurred consumers to become more health-conscious and increase their intake of vitamins and minerals such as vitamin C and zinc.

3. **Sustain new habits using contextual indicators.** Habits can form when a consumer begins associating a specific behavior with a particular context. Eventually, that behavior can become automatic. A contextual cue can be a specific task, time of day, or object placement. For example, hand sanitizer and disinfecting wipes should be kept near entryways.

4. **Align messages to consumer mindsets.** Connect with consumers in the moment. Recent events intensify people's emotions, making marketing tricky to navigate. Companies should, therefore, ensure that all their brand communications are in sync with consumer attitudes.

5. **Analyze consumer beliefs and behaviors.** Consumer beliefs and habits will continue to evolve rapidly. Companies must conduct primary consumer insights work (understanding and interpreting customer data) to comprehensively understand the changing consumer decision journey.

Companies rely heavily on broad age categories such as baby boomers, Gen X, millennials, and Gen Z as they devise new products and messaging campaigns. But when school children wear fashions that imitate what their Barbie dolls or Marvel comic heroes are wearing while octogenarians run marathons, it might be time to rethink whether these groupings are still useful. See Figure 63.

Suppose businesses want to make their products and services available to each generation in the best way possible. In that case, they need to adapt their brand experience to accommodate all the options that these groups rely on. The next generation will be different and may result from disruption.

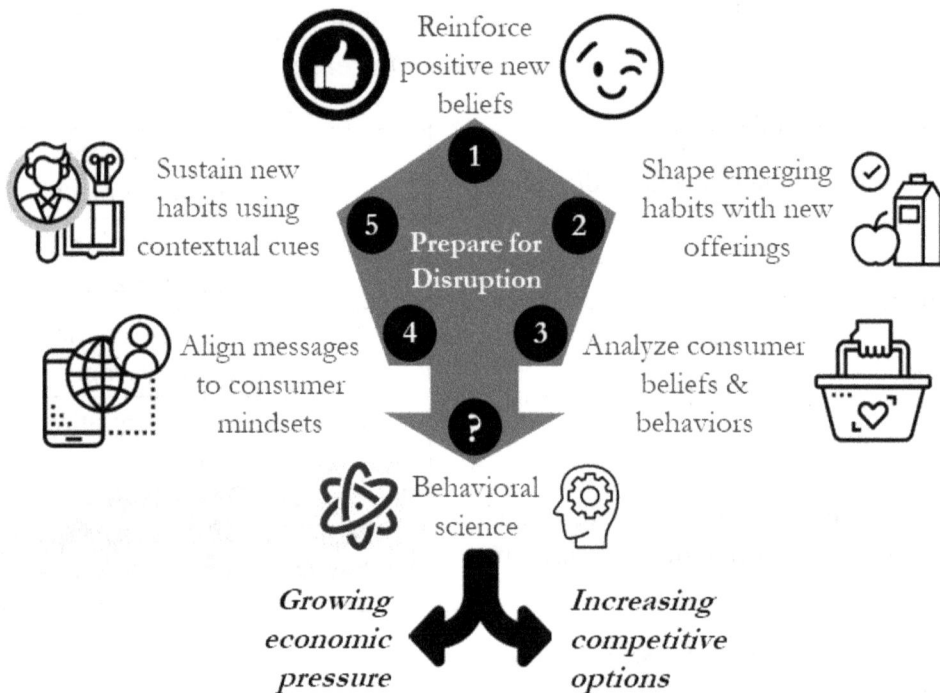

Figure 63: Preparation Actions Handling Disruption

Changing Customer Behavior & Expectations. Each generation has its own defining political and cultural traits that have characterized its buying habits. These generations respond uniquely when confronted with marketing tactics and purchasing preferences.

Solution. The first step to coping with disruption resulting from customers changing their behavior and expectations is to gather data, analyze signals, and know yourself, your organization, your industry, and your community.

Behavioral science tells us that identifying consumers' new beliefs, habits, and "peak moments" is central to driving behavioral change. Some actions can help companies influence consumer behavior in the long term. Thereby predicting disruption.

Contrary to conventional wisdom, the consumer has not been fundamentally rewired. The modern consumer is a construct of growing economic pressure and increasing competitive options.

The consumer is changing. They are more capricious and less loyal. They have less time but are more conscientious. They shy away from stores and prefer experiences over products.

Summary. Companies that develop a nuanced understanding of the changed beliefs, peak moments, and habits of their target consumer bases—and adjust their product offerings, customer experiences, and marketing communications accordingly—will be best positioned to thrive in the next normal. There are differences in consumer behavior across geographic markets and demographic groups. Consumers will remain cautious about resuming all their pre-disruption activities.

References & Bibliography.

1. Tamara Charm, "Understanding and shaping consumer behavior in the next normal," McKinsey; July 24, 2020
2. "How To Identify and Manage Disruptive Change," Indeed.com; March 29, 2021
3. "Changing Consumer Behavior," Bailey Brand Consulting
4. Kasey Lobaugh, "The consumer is changing," Deloitte Insights; May 29, 2019
5. Anne Jarry, "How much has consumer behavior changed in the past year," Marketing Tech; March 1, 2021
6. "How Each Generation Shops in 2020," Salesfloor; January 12, 2020

Category: Customer

Truth #17. You will face dissatisfied customers.

Background & Introduction. Customer experiences are changing all the time. In the last few years, we've seen massive changes in how consumers interact with brands - and what they've come to expect from those experiences. Today, people want and expect a full-service experience. They want a great product with all the bells and whistles and want to be simultaneously excited, delighted, and regarded as individuals. How can you provide this holistic and positive experience? See Figure 64.

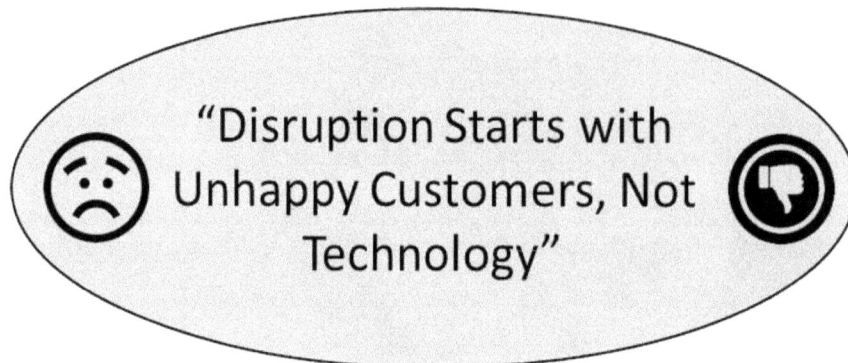

Figure 64: Dissatisfied Customer Quote

Dissatisfied customers are bad for business. Whether it's a product that doesn't work, a customer service representative who doesn't listen, or a company that makes promises they don't keep - unhappy customers will spread their dissatisfaction to everyone they know. When you don't satisfy your customers, then your customers develop a nonconstructive attitude towards your business. This faultfinding conduct compels the consumer to make negative comments about the business/product and take actions such as returning products not in line with how customers felt they were marketed. The overall effect is decreased customer loyalty and a general feeling of dissatisfaction.

Purpose. This chapter examines methods of managing outcomes resulting from dissatisfied customers. Figure 65 illustrates the challenge for a business experiencing this type of disruption.

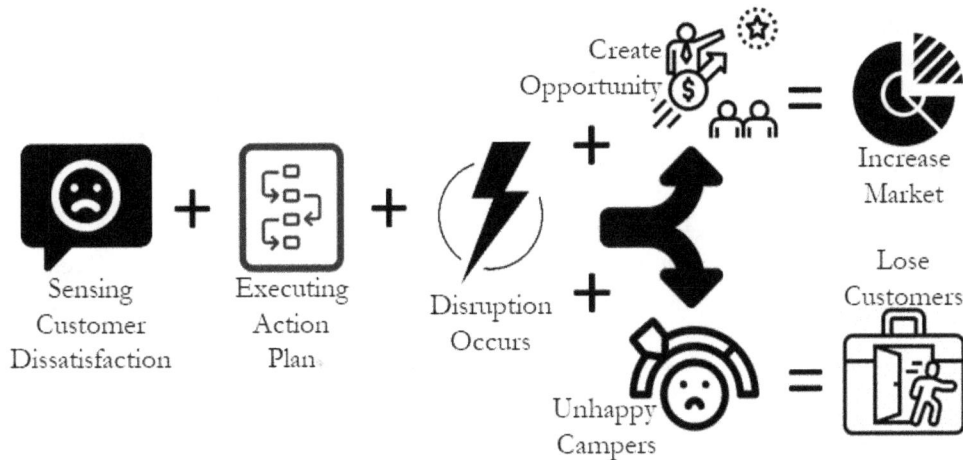

Figure 65: Dissatisfied Customer Disruption Challenge

Challenges. What causes customer dissatisfaction? It's a question every business seeks to know because the answer is vital to improving customer satisfaction. There are two reasons why a customer can feel displeased with a product or service.

Customers don't feel it's worth their money—the product doesn't live up to its quality, or they've spent too many resources (time and money) that don't feel worth it.

False advertising, poor customer service, or insincere promises make customers feel cheated and deceived. See Figure 66.

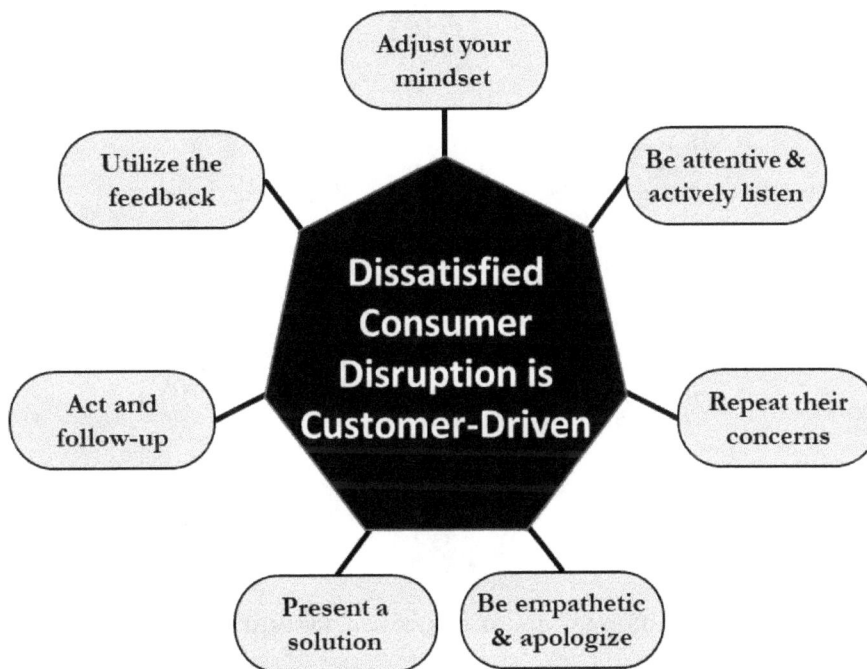

Figure 66: Dissatisfied Consumer Disruption is Customer-Driven

The causes of customer dissatisfaction result from a poor product and/or the inferior quality of your customer service. The challenge is to address customer dissatisfaction disruption by examining the customer experience. Customers want a fair product and enjoy the purchasing encounter.

Description. Customer dissatisfaction is a problem we often consider after the fact when it is too late to do anything about it.

The first step in avoiding this problem is to learn how to manage customer dissatisfaction before it happens. The next step is understanding what causes customer dissatisfaction and how to avoid it.

In most cases, unhappy customers are not a matter of bad luck; they can be managed and even avoided by paying attention and acting immediately.

After all, the best way to avoid disappointing customers is to keep their needs and expectations at the heart of your business model. There are reasons why this is happening. See Figure 67. The business culture has transformed in the following ways:

1. **Experience is the product.** In a way, experiences are products. People share their experiences with brands all the time. You want them to be positive. Control the customer reaction and the impact it has on your business. People are buying the whole experience as well as your product. Nurture positive experiences and act quickly on negative ones.
2. **All paths lead to the customer.** Create products or services that you think your customers need. However, talk to them first, collect feedback, and continuously improve your brand. Demonstrate the direct correlation between customer experience and sales growth.

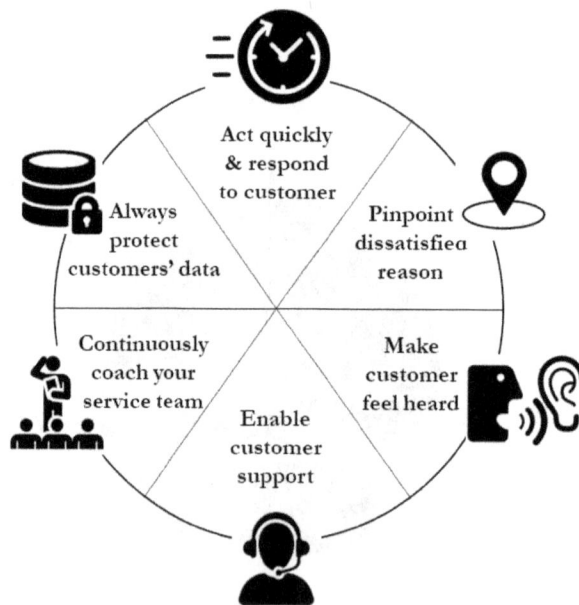

Figure 67: Suggestions to Improve Customer Experience

3. **Service is the new marketing.** Proactiveness and responsiveness to customer issues are the minimum standards; performing them humanely and being customer-focused are the keys. Your service people must buy into the idea of how important it is to provide an outstanding customer experience. This book suggests that workplace culture is critical -

happy and engaged employees provide good service. You want your customers to enjoy purchasing products and services from you. If you do, they will return again and again.

4. **Embracing tailored marketing through data.** Consumers will beat a path to the site that offers information on products that will be useful to them and help them satisfy their needs. To accomplish this correctly, you need to gather information about your audience. It is a continuous process because consumer tastes, needs, and desires constantly change. Here, we want to emphasize - protecting customer data; it is precious and should be treated as such.

5. **Customers demand real-time responsiveness.** Your business has a huge opportunity to leverage customer data to deliver individual experiences. This is not easy and requires attention to technology, employee skillsets, and product offering flexibility. Figure 67 provides suggestions to improve customer satisfaction and settle incidents promptly.

Solution. Complaints don't just spring out of thin air. They're the outcome of a long chain of events. The upside is an organization can dramatically decrease complaint volume by observing this process and finding ways to interrupt it before it ends in a dissatisfied customer or, worse, a group of angry customers. See Figure 68 for suggested steps in formulating a disruption action plan.

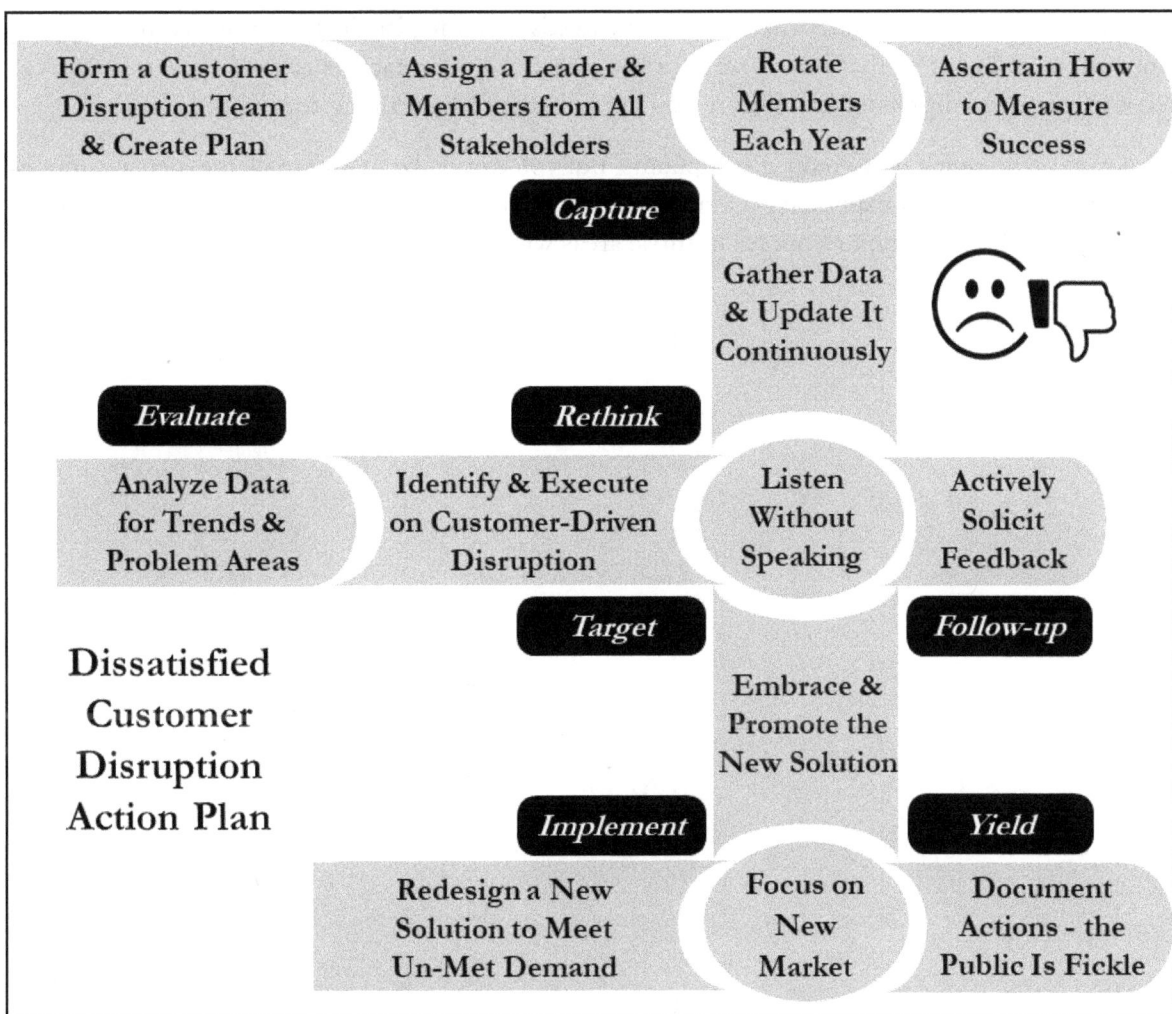

Figure 68: Proposed Disruption Action Plan for Dissatisfied Customers

Open all communication channels; don't shut down social media or block specific population segments. If a customer can contact your business at the first sign of trouble, minor frustrations are less likely to explode into costly, customer-upsetting, reputation-damaging grievances.

Set the tone. This is a cultural transformation. Even if you've provided proper customer service, your company culture or communication style might still send mixed signals to your customers.

Listen to the customer and other feedback, capture data and information, read/analyze it, and gain wisdom from it. If possible, turn the situation around and make a positive out of it. Turn the complaint into a product idea or empower your public relations with examples of quick response and resolution.

Reducing complaints involves the entire organization. It's about being proactive and reactive, taking preventative and remedial action. Dealing with difficult customers requires a special skill set. Hopefully, these recommendations will prepare you for dissatisfied customer disruption.

Summary. As time goes on and more of the customer experience gets automated, customer data will become even more critical. Without insights into your customers, businesses could find themselves with a product and/or service no one needs or wants, lackluster service compared to the competition, and content that shoots wide of the mark. All these factors can conspire to deliver a poor experience to the customer. Before you know it, they'll be walking for the door.

There may be no quick fix to reduce complaints, but you can make many small, inexpensive moves to improve the customer experience. Communication and team culture play a huge part in achieving customer pleasure. Investing resources in those areas will benefit the entire organization.

References & Bibliography.

Thales S. Teixeira, "Disruption Starts with Unhappy Customers, Not Technology," Harvard Business Review; June 06, 2019

"Dealing With Unhappy Customers - Communication Skills from Mind Tools," Mind Tools; February 28, 2022

Lawrence Ganti, "Why Disruption Begins with Unhappy Customers," Forbes; September 9, 2020

John Mehrmann, "10 Powerful Steps to Defuse Angry Customers," Business Know-How; September 11, 2020

Ron Kaufman, "What Are the Six Disruptors of Customer Experience," Uplifting Service; January 3, 2022

Nikky Lee, "Customer disruption_ 4 ways it can work for you," Perceptive; September 22, 2021

"How to manage customer dissatisfaction and what causes it," Kaizo; May 19, 2022

Brian j. Brim, Ed.D., and Jillian Anderson, "Strategies to Meet the Needs of Customers During Disruption," Gallup; June 23, 2020

Sabine Harnau, "How to reduce customer complaints sensibly and sustainably," Customer Sure; September 13, 2021

Category: External

Truth #18. Government activity will disrupt your operations.

Background & Introduction. Government activity impacts your business operations in all phases daily. As administrations come and go, new local and national leaders are elected, and American culture and public persona change; most organizations adjust their business practices accordingly. The company modifies activities deliberately because the change is anticipated, gradual, or has built-in lead time. On the other hand, disruption arrives swiftly. The impact is felt across several business operations at once. The disruption hits finances, supply chains, personnel, taxes, customers, the environment, and the cultural life of society. Recently, this has been occurring more often and with a more significant impact.

Environmental change, armed conflicts, worldwide pandemics, and endogenic (earthquakes, volcanos, etc.) factors will punch a business in its core. At first blush, the business leader says what can I do to get ready for fate, bad luck, an act of God, or the act of a madman? The fighter says, "We can do plenty to be prepared!" The survivor has a plan, calls it a disruption strategy, and is ready to execute it to meet challenges immediately and even turn a threatening set of events into a prospect.

Purpose. This chapter examines approaches for organizational leaders or governance boards to reach a reasonable and affordable readiness posture to elevate their preparedness for business disturbance. The approach centers around the CERTIFY methodology, which speaks to a proven framework for achieving this goal. Furthermore, this paper discusses this structure in context with unforeseen government activities that result in disruption.

Challenge. The high costs of natural catastrophes, acts of terrorism, and other disasters that can directly affect businesses are well known. As governments react in the interest of the country or constituency, they can trigger a piggyback disruption.

In the last decade alone, significant disruptions have resulted from:

- Political and social unrest.
- Cyber-attacks and technology failures.
- Pandemics and epidemics.
- Supply chain interruptions, including supplier bankruptcies.
- Port closures due to labor strikes.

- Loss of business stemming from terrorist attacks and mass shootings.
- Regulatory actions.
- Raw materials shortages
- Product recalls or contamination events

These events caused severe government reactions that affected businesses directly and indirectly. What is the role of government in the face of potentially disruptive change?

Governments establish the legal and regulatory systems that govern the economy's operation. They provide critical economic input by educating the public and providing public infrastructure and services. Governments also negotiate (through democratic processes) and maintain (through social expenditure and justice) an underpinning social compact with the community. Disruptive events and occurrences create implications (at times drastic) for each of these roles.

Solution. Adapting to change can be a big challenge for many businesses. However, as disruptive transformations turn many industries upside down, adaptability is increasingly essential for entrepreneurs. Change is the only constant in the business world. Government activities are changing how we work at a pace unseen before.

Governments are acclimating to disruption and forcing society to adapt (business and culture). We don't overcome disruption by being stronger or smarter than our competitors but by being better able to adapt to it. The steps below are things a business can do to prepare for disruption caused by government activities.

- **Let's keep it simple.** Consider disruption resulting from government activities using an impact effort matrix (IEM). The framework is shown in Figure 69.
- **Recognize the worth of adaptability.** Flexibility is crucial to being ready. The leader can't predict the disruption but can create the structure (personnel and structure) that survives and thrives.
- **Ascertain potential disruptors.** Create a dynamic list (updated frequently). Yes, even the list changes. Use your team (in-house & support) to fashion the impact effort matrix (IEM) that works for you. See Figure 69 at right.

Figure 69: Disruption IEM Example

- **Craft an early-warning system.** Identify the indicators. How will the organization sense that a red flag (threshold) has been breached? Recognize what needs to be in place to trigger automatically when disruption occurs.
- **Prepare a disruption plan.** The plan must be organization-wide, nurture understanding, encourage innovation, and emphasize risk/reward. This is a place where "outside the box" thinking is necessary. Evaluate and target these ideas and form them into action items.
- **Take small steps.** Tolerate failure. Learn. Every disruption has a learning curve and a lesson learned. Capture that data, all of it. Data is money!

Description. Businesses must navigate the financial and operational challenges of disruption while rapidly addressing the needs of their people, customers, and suppliers. Organizational leaders can turn massive complexity and business disturbance into meaningful change by taking the right actions.

Businesses must respond to the immediate impacts of one disruption, perhaps followed by another, and prepare for what comes next. The leadership group must execute responsible actions; see Figure 70. The process includes a continuous cycle of risk mobilization, early warning detection, urgent analysis, and prompt operation. These actions will help to optimize results and mitigate risks.

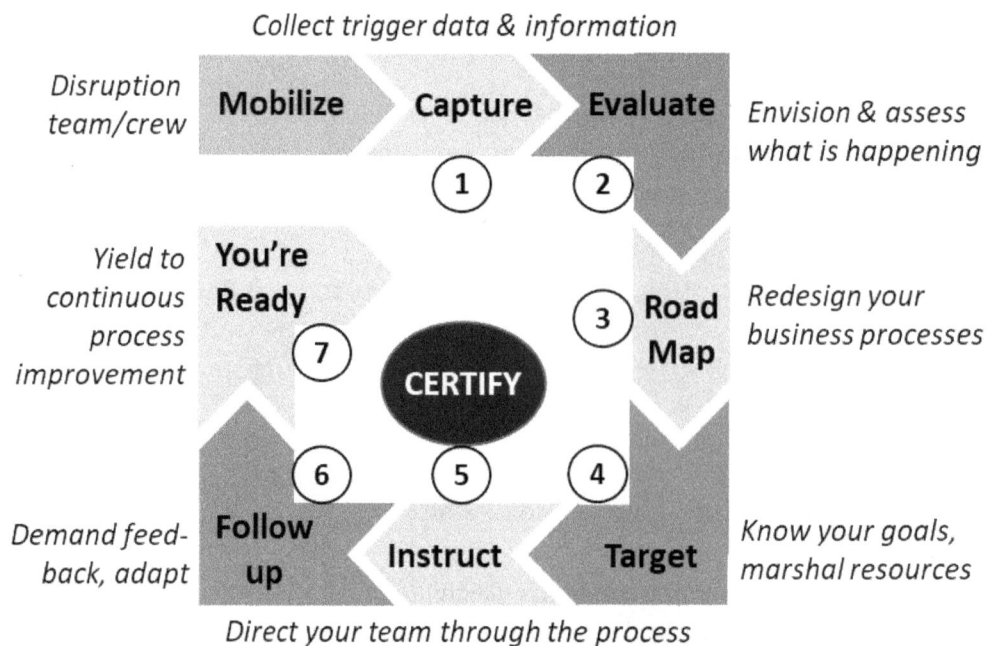

Collect trigger data & information

| Disruption team/crew | **Mobilize** ① | **Capture** | **Evaluate** ② | *Envision & assess what is happening* |

Yield to continuous process improvement — **You're Ready** ⑦ — **CERTIFY** — ③ **Road Map** — *Redesign your business processes*

Demand feed-back, adapt — **Follow up** ⑥ — **Instruct** ⑤ — **Target** ④ — *Know your goals, marshal resources*

Direct your team through the process

Figure 70: Disturbance Readiness Methodology

Actions. There are many directions that a business can embark upon when trying to improve disruption readiness. It is important to remember that these are unpredictable situations that arise. Thus, the best thing that can be done is to:

1. Have a disruption plan.
2. Assign disruption roles to your team.
3. Run scenarios through storyboard-like exercises.
4. Maintain cyber hygiene, inspect safety features, and safeguard emergency supplies.
5. Remain vigilant.
6. Train employees, including the leadership structure.
7. Consider insurance coverage.
8. Prepare a hotlist of front-page topics in the environment, politics, culture, arts, law enforcement, and business intelligence and review it each morning.

Most businesses are set up to react to direct physical damage but consider options that address many other disruption types. These include:

- Contingent business interruption coverage, which can protect against physical damage suffered by key suppliers.
- Cyber protection has evolved to cover not just data breaches but technology-driven business interruption.
- Political risk and trade credit financing can cover exposures related to government actions, instability, and insolvency.
- Non-damage business interruption policies (NDBI) can provide coverage for loss of revenue without a physical damage trigger.

Synopsis of Government Activities Disruption Biz Ops. Note the ways in which government activity can disrupt business operations. See Figure 71.

- **Regulatory Changes:** Governments often introduce new regulations or modify existing ones, which can increase compliance costs or restrict certain business practices. For example, stricter environmental regulations might force businesses to invest in costly equipment or change production processes.

- **Taxation:** Changes in tax laws, such as increases in corporate taxes or eliminating tax incentives, can directly impact a company's bottom line and financial planning.

- **Trade Policies**: Government decisions on trade agreements, tariffs, or import/export regulations can affect supply chains, pricing strategies, and market access for businesses involved in international trade.

- **Legal Proceedings:** Businesses may face legal challenges initiated by government agencies, such as antitrust investigations, intellectual property disputes, or lawsuits related to consumer protection.

- **Permits and Licenses:** Delays or denials in obtaining permits, licenses, or approvals from government agencies can hinder business expansion plans or delay project timelines.

- **Economic Policies:** Changes in monetary policy, interest rates, or government spending can influence consumer spending habits, inflation rates, and overall market conditions, impacting business performance.

- **Public Health Measures**: Government-imposed restrictions or mandates during public health crises, such as lockdowns, capacity limits, or vaccination requirements, can disrupt normal business operations, particularly in sectors like hospitality, tourism, and retail.

- **Labor Regulations:** Government policies related to labor standards, employment contracts, or immigration can affect workforce management, hiring practices, and business labor costs.

- **Subsidies and Incentives:** While government subsidies or incentives can benefit some businesses, they may also distort market competition and create unsustainable dependencies in the long term.

- **Nationalization or Expropriation:** In extreme cases, governments may seize private assets or industries through nationalization or expropriation, leading to significant disruptions for affected businesses.

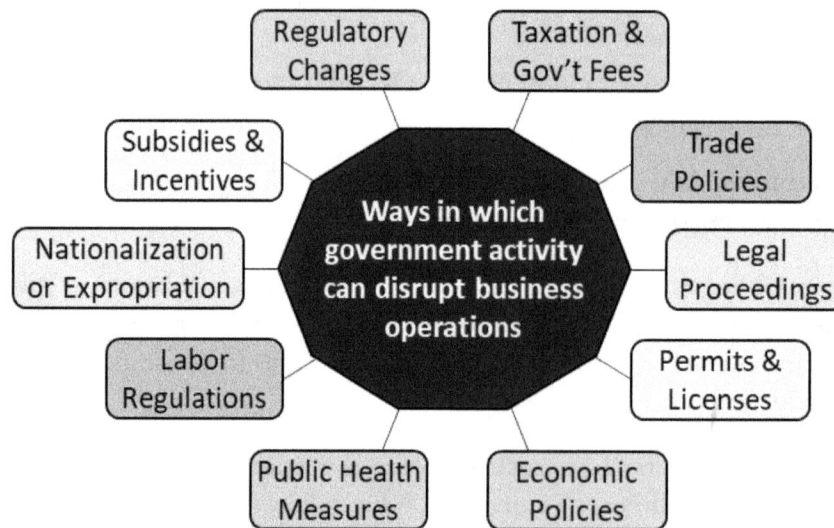

Figure 71: Ways Gov't Actions Impact Biz Ops

Summary. Businesses must urgently build long-term resilience in their value chains to manage future challenges. This requires holistic approaches to disruption management. Companies must build in sufficient flexibility to protect against future disruptions. They should also consider developing a robust framework that includes a responsive risk management operations capability.

That capability should strive to be technology-led, leveraging platforms that support applied analytics, artificial intelligence, and machine learning. It should also ensure end-to-end transparency across the company culture. In the long term, risk response must become an integral part of business-as-usual protocols. Become great at adapting quickly to disruption.

References and Bibliography.

1. "Monetary Policy Basics," Business Education University, 2019
2. "The Structure and Functions of the Federal Reserve System," Federal Reserve System; 2016
3. "How to respond to disruption," Accenture; 2021
4. "Business Interruption and Civil Authority Insurance," Rock Fusco & Connelly; Mar 25, 2016"
5. "Business Interruption: Looking Beyond the Physical," Marsh & Company; April 12, 2022
6. "5 steps to prepare your business for future disruption," BDC CEO Excellence Retreat, 2020

Category: External

Truth #19. The economy will turn sour.

Background & Introduction. Since the first caveman sharpened a stone into a tool, economics has involved disruption. New technologies create innovative ways of doing business and displace old ones.

The key to progress is ensuring that there are more winners than losers from economic disruptive change and that the losers survive and benefit from the industry's gains in success.

An economic disruption is when markets cease to function regularly, typically characterized by rapid and significant market declines. Market disruptions can result from physical threats to the stock exchange or unusual trading (as in a crash). Numerous factors generate these wide swings. Upon analysis, the unfortunate was found to be unprepared for disruption.

Economic disruption occurs when a company creates a new segment in an existing market to reach unserved or underserved customers—for example, creating a cheap version of an expensive product to satisfy less-wealthy consumers. This causes the economy to "sour" for some organizations.

The beauty of the disruption economy is that it enables two opportunities. First, it allows companies to redefine how and why they work. Such an organizational awakening leads to the second opportunity for companies to adopt a technology innovation or grab a new market by producing more efficiently.

Phygital (physical plus digital) is a marketing term that describes blending digital experiences with physical ones. For an economic example, see Figure 72.

With disruption comes the opportunity for eruption—the closing of one door and the innovative opening of another—the opportunity to create and proliferate and wither and die if it "sours."

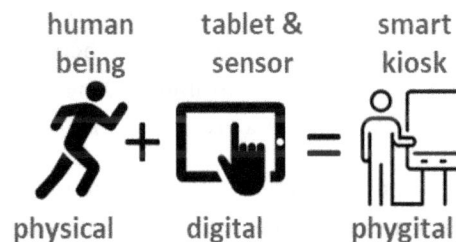

Figure 72: Components of Phygital

The point is that the knowledge-sharing economy opens the door to exponentially greater opportunities for innovation. Nobody is more intelligent than everybody, and the same is true when looking outward from one's organization rather than inward. Open social media has given companies a method for learning from other companies.

Purpose. This chapter discusses preparation steps companies can adopt before the economy turns downward at the organizational, community, industry, and/or national levels. It also provides suggestions to assist businesses in preparing for disruption and seizing a growth opportunity should it present itself.

Challenge. The term disruption often connotes negativity, as if the change associated with disruption is bad. It isn't always. It's an opportunity that depends on the company's readiness to innovate, change, and embrace a new process, market, technology, and/or culture.

New in 'disruption' is the intelligence (from data-driven analysis), the speed of technology, and the pace at which businesses must adopt, adapt, and innovate to survive. This is the challenge presented by the disruption caused by "the economy will turn sour." See Figure 73.

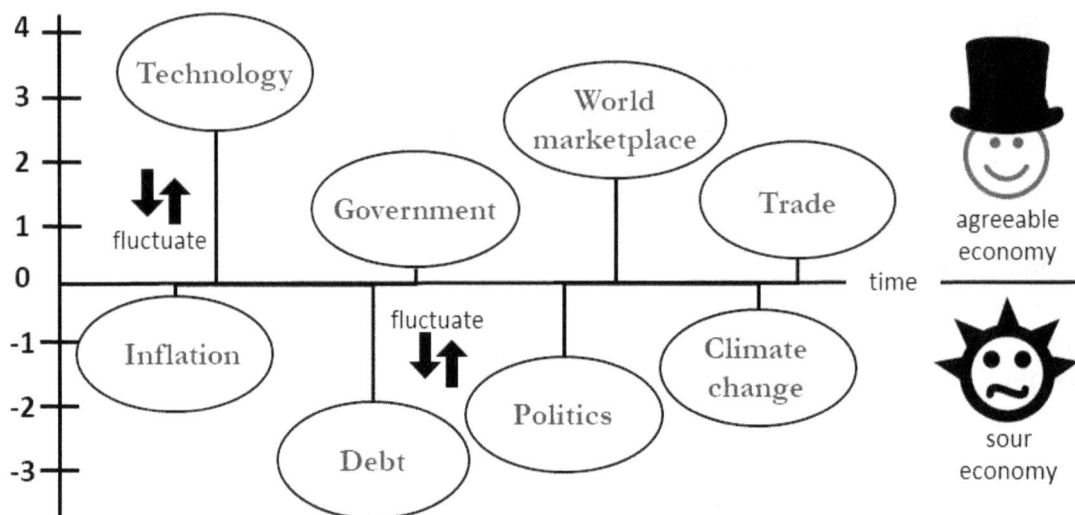

Figure 73: Factors to Consider that Impact the Economy

Description. The power of today's disruptive economy is noticeably real. Disrupters such as Amazon can take down market shares with a simple announcement. For example, the needle moved on cryptocurrency value when Tesla announced they were accepting cryptocurrency as payment for their automobiles. When Amazon announced its intent to enter the prescription drug market, CVS' and Walgreens' stocks plummeted.

Digital transformation trends shape business and society, adding complexity to innovative organizations' challenges. To survive and thrive, companies must be prepared to address each. Seven of these trends are listed below and shown in Figure 74.

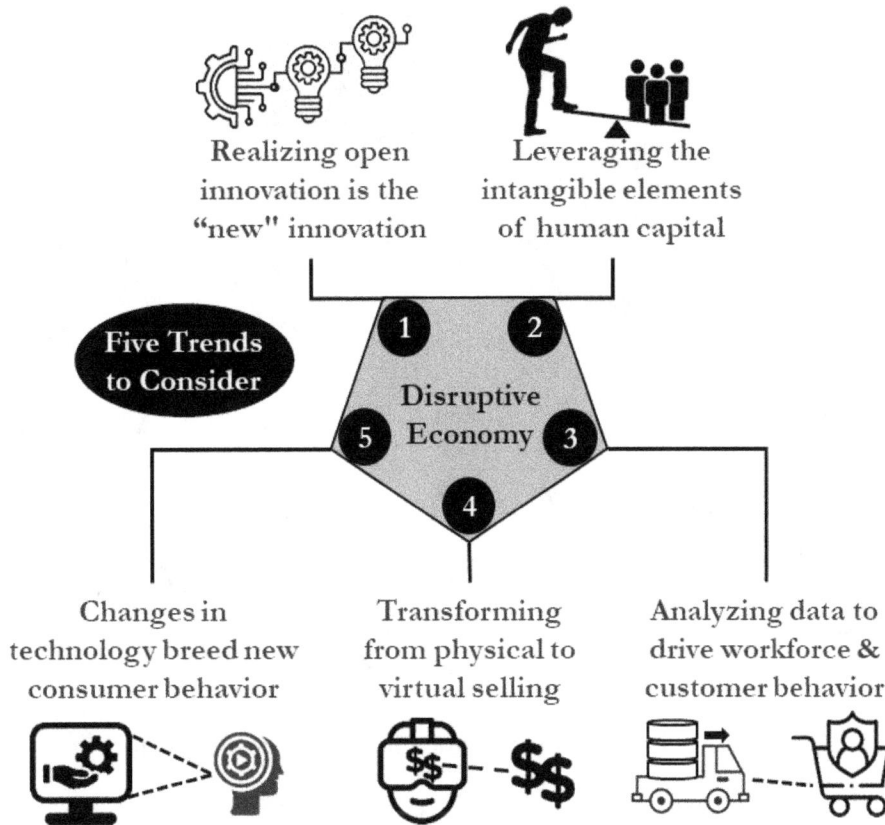

Figure 74: Five Trends that Cause a Disruptive Economy

The Transformed Economy has been Disrupted. Consumers want flawless and personalized omnichannel experiences. Companies develop new, innovative ways to serve and delight customers. In turn, consumers adapt to new novelties and turn them into demands, prompting businesses to reconstruct or recreate something new to transform their business's successful environment.

Partnership Ecosystems. This partnership was created to add value to products and services by combining resources and products. It truly reflects that the combined value is greater than the sum of the individual partners' contributions. This value is expressed not only in exceptional customer experiences but also in outstanding partner experiences.

Phygital Experiences. A phygital encounter (see Figure 75) combines in-person experiences with digital convenience. Today's public desires the best of both. Omnichannel now means every channel, including the physical channel (face-to-face). Significantly, delivering phygital experiences relies on knowing the customer at every point of performance and ensuring exceptional service with personal privacy and cyber hygiene.

IoT, IIoT, and OT Devices. The Internet of Things, industrial IoT, and operational technology have exploded onto the market. Most items can now be controlled from your smartphone. Refrigerators, room lighting, and physical mirrors make life more convenient.

Cybercrime and Overreach. The downside is that most of these devices are not secure, and they increase the cyber-attack surface, and the bad guys are taking advantage of that.

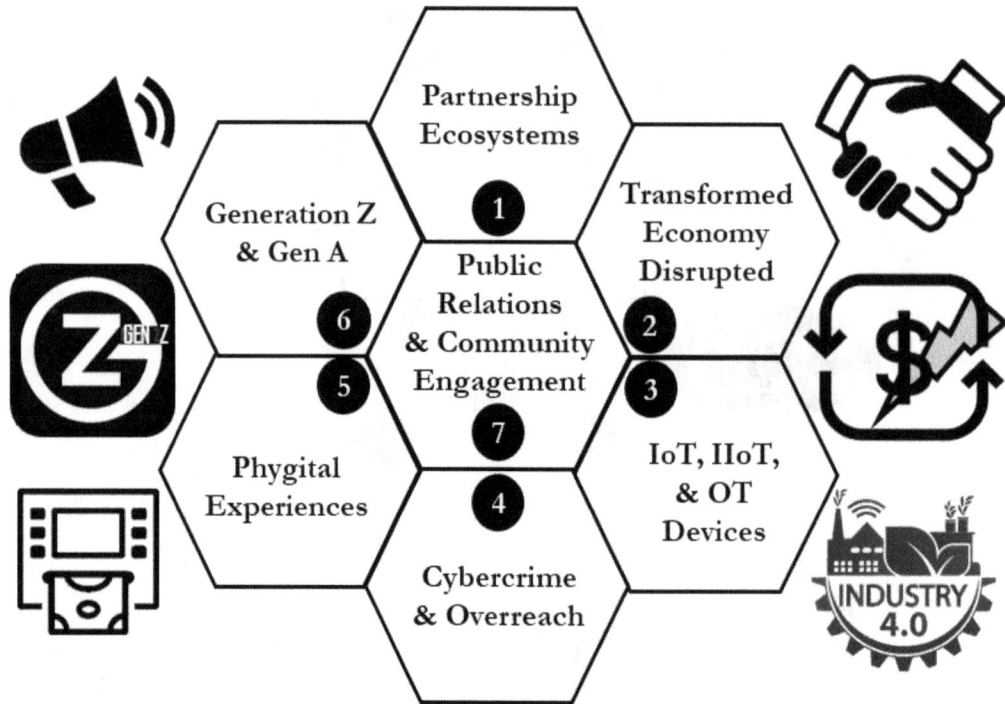

Figure 75: Areas of Importance for Economic Disruption

Nothing is more disheartening to a company than finding out that their data has been ransomed or their supply chain has been shut down. While progress has been made within the past few years, justice has often fallen short of the public's expectations.

Public Relations & Community Engagement. Society has reached an age of distrust. People are keenly aware of the data-collecting capabilities of social media giants and search engines and of selling their personal information. The population is now driving corporate governance (transparency and regulations). Consumers are demanding more protection and control.

Generation Z & Gen A. Marketing consultants claim that Generation Z is now the largest generation, constituting 32% of the global population and surpassing the millennials and Baby Boomers. Companies prepared for disruption are already examining ways to improve their organization's readiness. They have labeled the members of Gen Z as digitally native. Born from 1995 to 2010, they have been exposed to the internet, social networks, and smartphones. Gen Z and Gen Alpha are loyal to experiences rather than to brands.

Solution. The graphic in Figure 76 provides a suggested action plan for economic disruption.

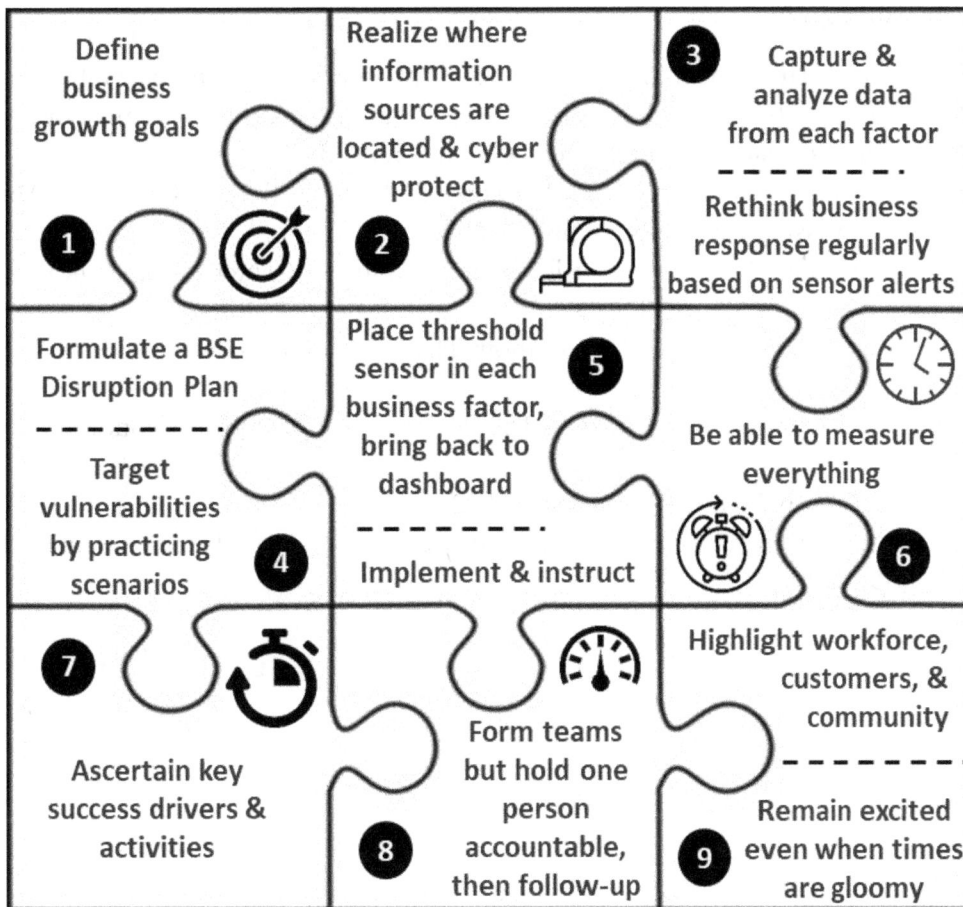

Figure 76: Elements of a Successful Disruption Plan for a Sour Economy

Every company's leadership should understand the essential elements of its Business Success Ecosystem (BSE) and make decisions about optimizing its operational efficiency and market impact while being mindful of what drives its organization's engine.

Summary. An unusual combination of factors, characterized by a prolonged labor shortage, supply chain disruptions, and chaos in the energy market, caused economic disruption. These events make it more difficult to predict where the economy is heading. This chapter discusses several steps progressive companies can take to prepare for economic disruption. Coupled with a disruption plan that includes monitoring markers in each significant factor of the economy, it improves the chances of weathering a major disturbance or catastrophe. It begins with gathering information about your products, customers, industry, and community. Create scenarios, assign key personnel, and practice. Perhaps your organization will thrive when the economy turns sour.

References & Bibliography.

1. Brennen Jensen "What's happening with the American economy right now," Hub; June 8, 2020
2. Marsh McLennan, "WEF_The_Global_Risks_Report_2022," World Economic Forum; 2022
3. Walter Frick, "Is a recession coming," Quartz; April 13, 2022
4. Tim Smart, "Consumers Sour Slightly on Economy in April but Remain Optimistic About the Future," U.S. News & World Report; April 26, 2022
5. Matthew P. Goodman, "Economics Is All About Disruption," Center for Strategic and International Studies; May 28, 2020
6. Jeff Boss, "5 Things You Need To Know About The Disruption Economy," Forbes Magazine; November 23, 2015
7. Shasta Turney, "Disrupt or Be Disrupted - The Power of the Disruptive Economy," ForgeRock; September 9, 2019
8. "Eight Transformation Trends," ForgeRock; 2022
9. Stuart Ayling, "Economy turning sour_ Find the sweet spot for your business," LinkedIn; March 12, 2019

Category: External

Truth #20. Geopolitical events will influence behaviors.

Background & Introduction. Historical intelligence and traditional and organizational structures are useless to disruption planning leaders. To thrive, companies must adapt their cultures and strategies to survive regular disruption and profit from it. Different scenarios may impact consumer demand, business outlook, and market behavior. Figure 77 provides a graphic showing eight scenarios that could disrupt the World and influence behaviors. Two or more events may form a hybrid disruption, making matters worse.

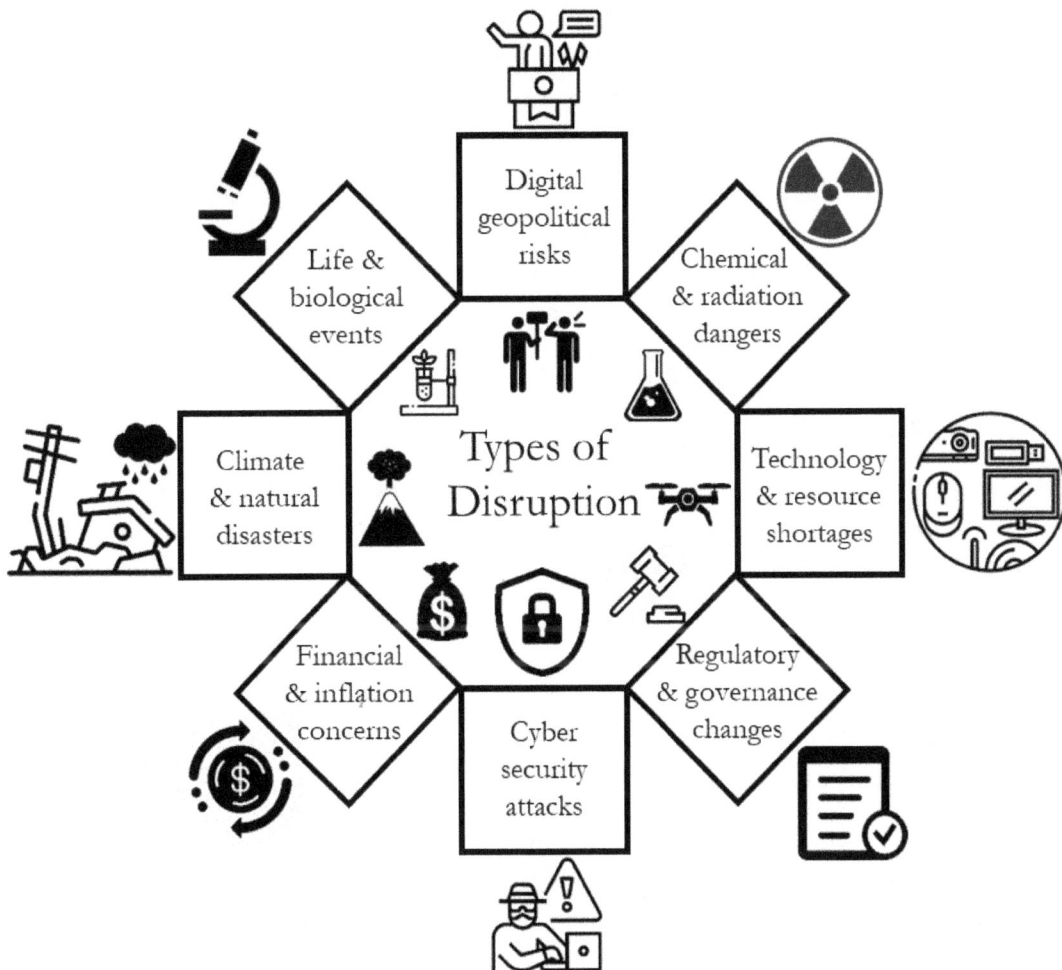

Figure 77: Types of Disruption Related to Geopolitical Risk and Other World Events

Geopolitics and technology are inseparably interconnected in today's geostrategic ecosystem, but many business leaders who concentrate on digital transformation do not consider digital geopolitical risk.

The geopolitics of technology and data is a top risk affecting states and companies across all sectors and geographies. While business leaders recognize the impact technology and digital innovation have on their companies, they ignore the impact of digital geopolitical uncertainty. Organizations should incorporate four key geopolitical threats into their digital technology strategy and risk management approaches.

1. Evolving technology policies & regulations
2. Cybersecurity threats
3. Industrial policy barriers
4. Increasing geostrategic competition

World events and digital geopolitical risk are among the most unsettling trends facing business and state leaders today. The increasing significance of innovative data systems has given digital geopolitics its unique class of disruption.

Geostrategy is the geographic direction of a state's foreign policy. More precisely, it describes where an organization concentrates its energies by controlling the flow of information, projecting military power, and directing political activity. This approach is vital to industry leaders with international holdings and markets. Any natural disaster or localized conflict is measured in geopolitical risk.

Purpose. This chapter aims to describe and alert business leaders to the disruptive trend of digital political uncertainty combined with world events. Governments are increasingly exploring how to control their populations by controlling information. To accomplish this, leaders must use digital technology to control data capture, flow, storage, and movement. These significant world-class disturbances are complicated to prepare for and even more difficult to predict. Then, it is problematic to forecast suitable and/or mitigating responses after occurrence. This chapter discusses when world events influence behaviors during disruption, and responses become more complex when digital political uncertainty is involved.

Challenge. Digital geopolitical risk is a dangerous disruption because of the power of information. Those who control the data control information, and those who control people are the organizations that succeed. This presents all business, government, and societal leaders with a challenge that requires preparation.

Adapting to and embracing these disruptions goes against human nature. Many resist change and uncertainty and resort to fear, ambiguity, and doubt. Sensationalism, exaggeration, and a lack of clarity between fact and fiction can amplify this. This is part of the geopolitical challenge when coping with world-class disruption.

Description. In the aftermath of significant disruptions, two viewpoints emerge, suggesting that (1) "life" will return to normalcy once the dust settles or that (2) everything will permanently change. Recent history shows that these events trigger changes that can be perpetuated for long periods. Sometimes, system-wide changes impose new barriers, changing how businesses prioritize solutions.

What are examples of geopolitical risk and their intrinsic disruption? Five strategies are described below. When reading them, spotlight two relative concerns that are impacted by these types of disruption and ultimately become methods of control. These concerns are public perception, society and culture, and the information fed to the population. See Figure 78.

Expropriation. Governments can confiscate assets, nationalize property, breach contracts, impose embargoes, or prohibit trade with specific countries. The government expropriates many of these companies, and foreign firms need to conduct additional due diligence to determine their relationships with partners, society, and the government.

Regulatory Burdens. Governments can discriminate against foreign firms by imposing stringent regulatory requirements, limiting foreign direct investment, and allowing domestic industry monopolies to form. Unstable regimes or upcoming elections may also pose a risk.

Violence and Civil Unrest. Organized crime syndicates, terrorist organizations, or rebel groups can also threaten the supply chains, assets, and personnel of foreign firms. Protesters specifically targeted some foreign firms and were highly disruptive to the business operations of those foreign firms.

Cultural Missteps. Careless efforts to understand the social and cultural dynamics of the communities in which foreign firms operate and superficial attempts to engage local stakeholders can quickly turn into biases and resentment and lead to boycotts, protests, demonstrations, and negative media attention.

Human Rights Violations. Operations in countries with poor human rights records can cause supply chain disruptions. Still, they can also lead to reputational damage and give rise to class action lawsuits, public boycotts, or stockholder divestment campaigns.

Geopolitics describes the **geographic influences** on power relationships in international relations. The resulting competition between nations plays out in many economic, military, and societal areas.

Due to the increasing importance that **digital technology** plays in each of these areas, digital geopolitics is emerging as a unique category of impact. Business leaders must play a pivotal role in assessing corporate risk and redesigning digital systems. Four considerations are listed below.

Protect digital sovereignty. Digital sovereignty will be a primary source of complex, dynamic & expanding compliance obligations for multinational enterprises.

Figure 78: Five Approaches to Geopolitical Risk & Uncertainty

Build a local technology industry. The technology industry is of great interest to public policymakers due to its size, fast growth, strategic importance, tax revenue, & employment possibilities. Many national governments are investing in developing a home-grown tech sector.

Achieve necessary military capability. The emerging sphere of cyberwarfare and the digitalization of existing warfighting and security technologies impact enterprises.

Exert direct control over the governance of cyberspace. National competition for control over cyberspace governance will impact the operations of multinational enterprises as digital technology weaves itself through all aspects of society.

Solution. The suggestions listed below and shown in Figure 79 will assist the organization leader in preparing for geopolitical uncertainty and world event disruption that has an extensive impact on the population of citizens and customers.

1. **Develop** an intimate knowledge of diverse, complex, and developing geopolitical dynamics.
2. **Identify** challenges and recognize potential risks before they become disruptions.
3. **Make** recommendations to manage, mitigate, and respond to geopolitical disruption.
4. **Conduct** geopolitical due diligence before entering an emerging or volatile market.
5. **Complete** homework before forming a business partnership with a company in dicey jurisdictions.
6. **Rethink** competing in areas known for widespread corruption, civil unrest, human rights violations, and reneging on agreements.
7. **Calculate** a Digital Geopolitical Risk Index (DGRI) as a baseline and reference point to compare to previous or other geopolitical environments.
8. **Realize** a deeper and more granular understanding of the threats to controlling the information and the situation.

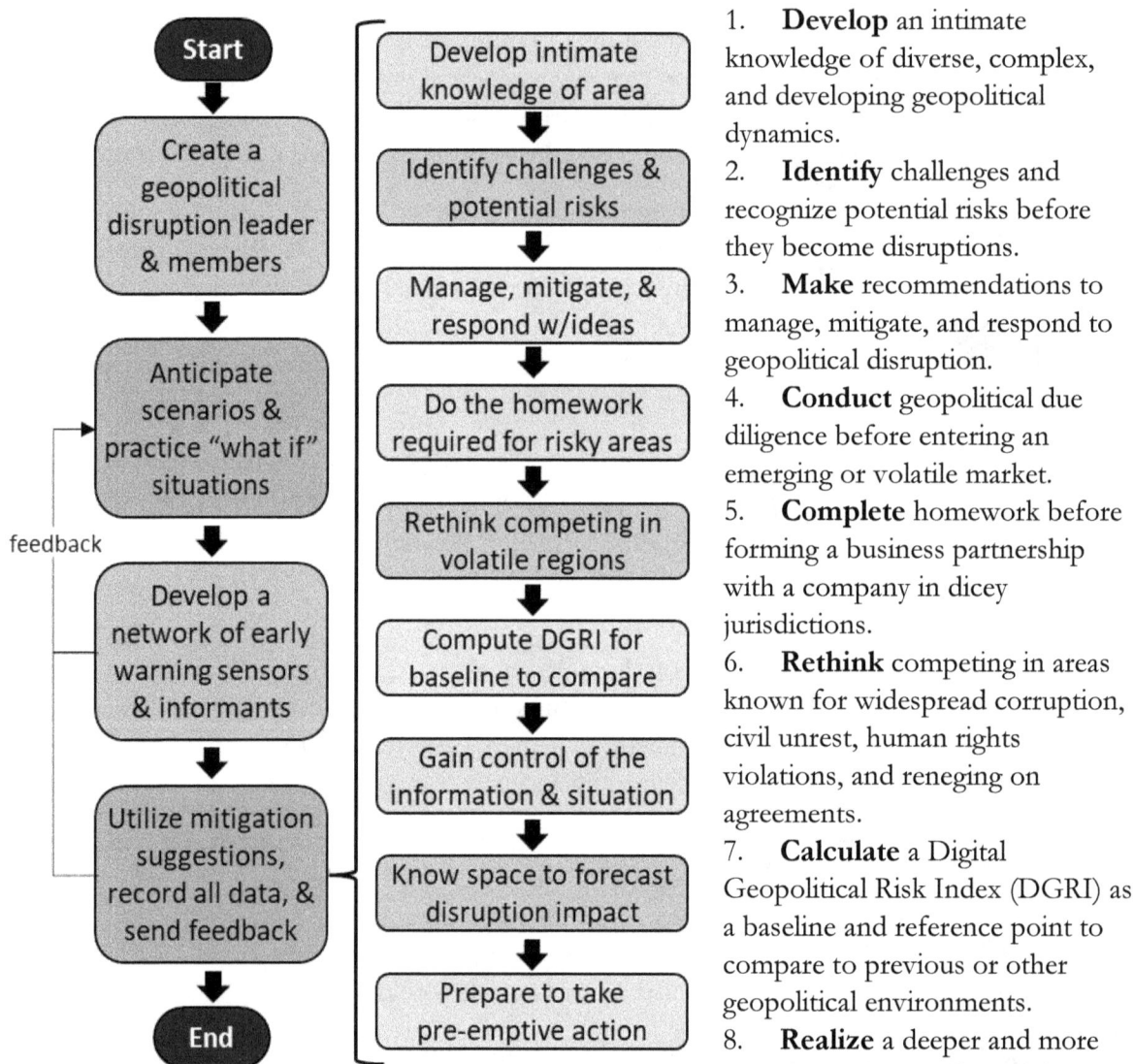

Figure 79: Mitigating Digital Geopolitical Risk & the effects of World Class Disruption

10. **Understand** the landscapes and inherent risks associated with the company industry in that area. This will enhance the ability to forecast disruption type, probability, and impact on business operations.
11. **Prepare** the business leader to take pre-emptive action to improve business decisions, protect assets and personnel, and mitigate risk exposure.

Tailor geopolitical risk assessments to focus on target markets, companies, population, culture, & government. The organization will also support readiness preparations by performing a digital geopolitical risk evaluation. Figure 80 and the steps below provide a blueprint for accomplishing this effort. Conducting valuable geopolitical due diligence can:

a. Examine political uncertainty during elections and/or regime change.
b. Ascertain discriminatory government actions restricting business operations.
c. Underscore control mechanisms affecting foreign investors, such as barriers of entry, regulatory changes, or limits to foreign direct investment.
d. Appraise levels of corruption in the public & private sectors & the judiciary.
e. Investigate foreign relations with neighbors, competitors, trade partners, and the international community.
f. Scrutinize the stability of the economy.
g. Explore key infrastructure & access to communication, healthcare, labor, & utilities.
h. Probe local perceptions of foreign operators.
i. Understand industry stakeholders and their relations with key domestic, government, and international actors.
j. Provide intelligence, analysis, and insight into security threats facing the client's people, assets, and operations.
k. Consider the area's record for the preservation of human rights.

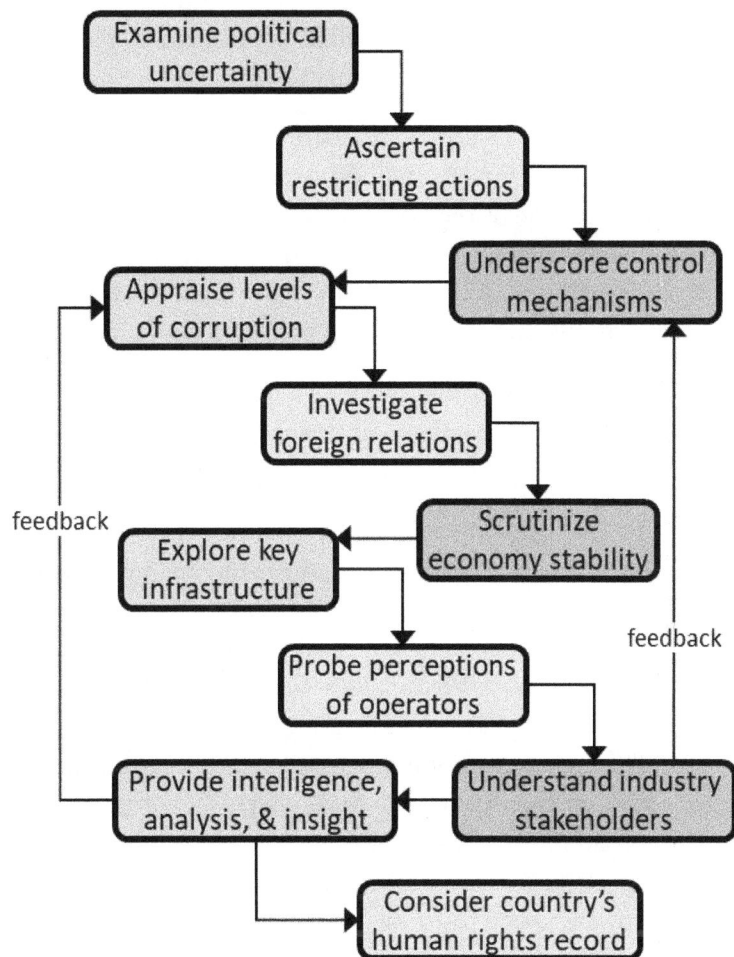

Figure 80: Ideas for a Digital Geopolitical Risk Evaluation

Resolution. Additional suggestions and recommendations for disruption preparation are shown below. Thinking in advance prepares your organization for disturbances of all kinds. Scenario planning and storyboarding go a long way toward putting pieces in place when disruption occurs.

Set the playing field. Preparing for disruption begins with assigning a disruption planner and team. Ensure the company culture supports disruption readiness; this is very important. This requires a mindset for all stakeholders to think and then rethink. Formulate a disruption plan; use the suggestions below as example steps.

Much of the competitive and market intelligence, customer insights, market dynamics, global economic scenarios, and all related intelligence & insights from only a few weeks ago no longer apply to most anticipated scenarios. Additionally, the speed of disruption is accelerated by business uncertainty, consumer fear, and difficulty discerning fact from fiction. From this, a common truth rises to the top.

Lead through never-ending disruption. Gaining a competitive advantage requires disruption planners to regard almost every day as a potentially highly disruptive scenario and improve their readiness to handle disruption. Organizations should establish a robust plan to embrace the impending disruption. This is key to disruption preparedness and requires continuous, seamless integration between data capture and assessment and continuously rethinking behaviors. Then, one can focus on the target even though it is constantly moving.

Not all uncertainty is the same. There is relentless data uncertainty that remains to be discovered during disruption preparation. It depends on the outcome of circumstances outside the organization's control (e.g., government policy, performance of new technology, or natural disaster). One way to look at this is to recognize that uncertainty falls into four categories. See Figure 81.

1. Level 1 scenario suggests that the uncertainty is small enough that a general forecast based on analytics and known parameters can be reasonably evaluated with the least risk.
2. The level 2 scenario realizes that the environment is a bit more complex and uncertainty is higher. Probability factors assist in determining the likelihood of which scenario might play out given various outcomes.
3. The level 3 environment grasps that little is known about the outcome; trends or patterns may emerge from traditional analyses. Disruption planners use Predictive Analytics to design a roadmap and solution.
4. Level 4 is a worst-case scenario; it is impossible to ascertain potential outcomes. All the variables need to be identified, which could amplify the degree of uncertainty even more.

Build the company to withstand uncertainty. The uncertainty levels and the corresponding course of action are only one step in the disruption planning methodology. The proactive business leader has adopted an appropriate organizational structure and adapted a culture and mindset taught throughout the company. This corresponds with a pre-emptive approach to disruption resolution. Often, a significant world disruption, natural disaster, or armed conflict is the trigger that explodes onto the scene. Forecasting this is next to impossible; however, preparations can be made.

Disruptions are here to stay. Since the fourth Industrial Revolution has taken a foothold in business economics, disruptions take hold quickly, are highly impactful, and are essentially continuous. Task the disruption team with a means to trend spot to quickly assess rapid shifts in business sector direction, technology usage, or supply chain sourcing.

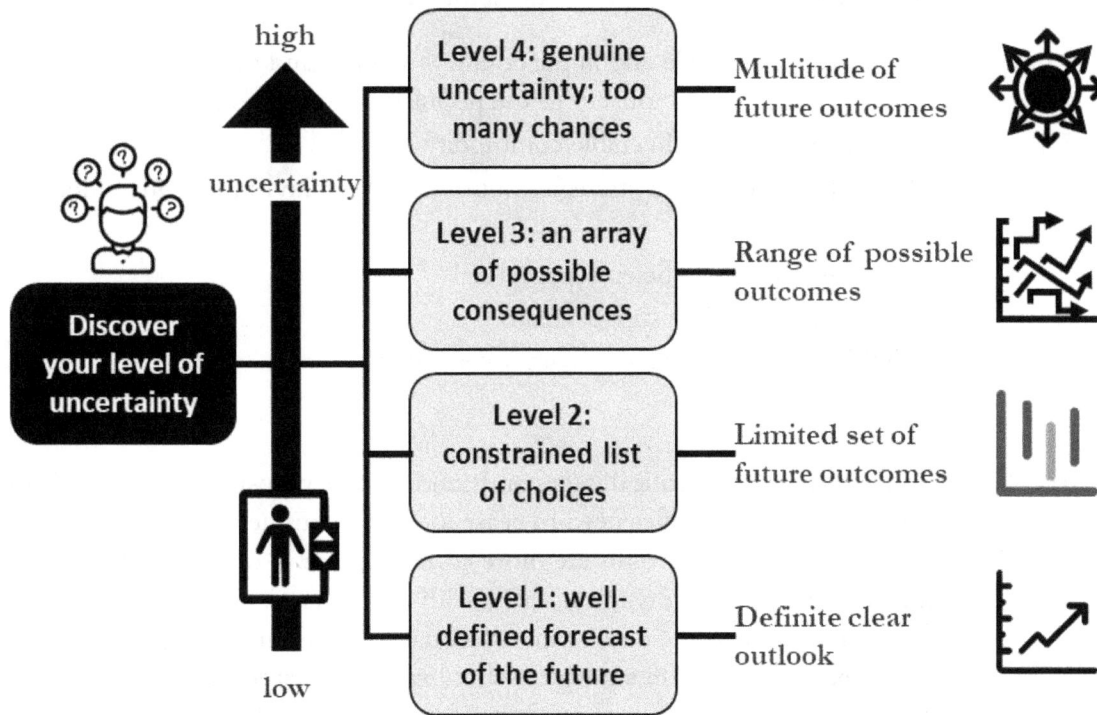

Figure 81: Uncertainty Levels

Situational awareness is contagious. Scenario planning is an excellent way to gain perspective on tactics that were not previously considered. It can highlight areas ripe for change and disruption. Scenario Planning must be generated and played out on multiple time horizons, segmented by business function. Capture forward-looking intelligence, create scenarios, and recognize options. This is a continuous process, exercised each day. See Figure 82.

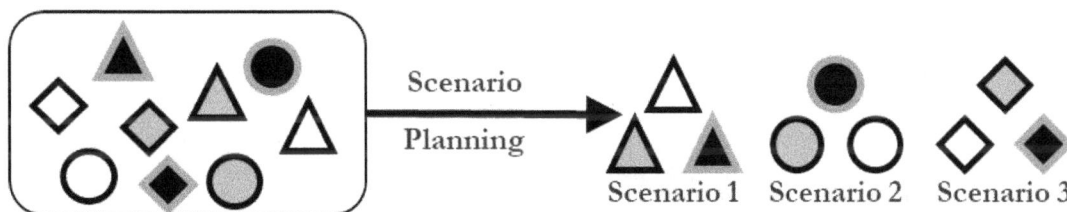

Figure 82: Scenario Planning is Crucial to Disruption Planning

Collecting information and applying analysis tools is automatic. Data gathering must be performed as frequently as possible. In the current environment, new content is generated every day.

This dynamic information is scrutinized continuously to effectively grasp predictive outcomes and resulting roadmaps.

Organizational preparedness is fundamental. Additionally, organizations must maintain flexibility to pivot quickly from one operating model to another. Activities include:

- Know the environment worldwide and in the country. Understand the market, culture, governance policies, and their relationship to the population and customer base.
- Transition to core services as a deliverable commodity
- De-commit clauses for efficient exit strategies out of long-term investment guarantees
- Allow self-managed work hubs
- Commission your R&D teams to be entrepreneurial
- Implement flexible and redundant supply chains
- Manufacture nimbleness on product configurations and features

Summary. This chapter has addressed critical issues and actions to help business leaders reframe the future of their organizations. Companies need to cease looking at business disruptions as singular events. Today, highly disruptive events are more commonplace. Companies that refuse to recognize this fundamental fact risk their organizational health and survival. We should remember that digital geopolitical technology is at the core of international relations and strategic competition. Countries have expanded export controls in strategic technologies and restricted market access for other companies in the telecommunications and semiconductor industries. They are emphasizing that this assists the national interest in governing the information flow to the citizens.

References & Bibliography.

1. Susan Moore, "Gartner Says Geopolitical Risk Will Provide CIOs New Leadership Opportunities," Gartner Press Release; August 24, 2022
2. Christofer Dehn & Nicholas Everington, "Geopolitical Risk – What Is It and How Can Companies Respond to It," Kroll; January 21, 2020
3. Courtney Rickert McCaffrey and Oliver Jones, "How to factor geopolitical risk into technology strategy," EY Global; February 18, 2022
4. Dale Buckner, "How to Better Prepare for the Next Global Disruption," Global Guardian; 2021
5. Aptean team, "6 Global Events That Disrupted the Manufacturing Supply Chain," Aptean; September 20, 2021
6. "The 11 Kinds of Event Disruption Planners Must Watch Out For _ ITA Group," ITA Group: October 23, 2021
7. Scott D. Anthony and David S. Duncan, "The Big-Event Disruption Playbook" Innosight; April 8, 2020
8. Resha P. Leasing, "Historical events and Supply Chain Disruption Chemical, Biological, Radiological, and Cyber Events," University of Michigan; 2003
9. Maurico Blas, "A Framework for Designing Supply Chain Disruptions," ResearchGate; March 14, 2018
10. David Potter, "A history of disruption, from fringe ideas to social change," Aeon Essays; December 23, 2021
11. Paul Santilli, "Global Disruptions are the New Norm, So Businesses Better Get Used To It," SCIP; June 2, 2020
12. Jacques Bughin and Jonathan Woetzel "Global trends: Navigating a world of disruption," McKinsey; January 22, 2019
13. Valeria Nyu, "Strategies for Coping with Global Disruptions: Diversify, Transform, Disengage, or Bypass," Rutgers Business Review; October 7, 2020

Category: External

Truth #21. Weather will affect your operations.

Background & Introduction. What can businesses do to mitigate the impact of Weather disruptions like floods, hurricanes, or earthquakes? How do companies keep their employees safe while also minimizing business disruption? How does an organization plan and prepare for a weather disruption to ensure a rapid response and recovery?

Companies have long engaged in risk assessment and mitigation as a core business practice. Heavy precipitation, heat waves, and droughts have increased over the last half-century. Businesses may not have a position on climate change. Still, they understand how a flood can shut down transportation, a hurricane can topple buildings and powerlines, or extreme temperatures can disrupt markets and threaten operations and supply chains.

Companies have always navigated a changing business environment. But now they face a changing physical environment, as climate change leads to more frequent and intense heat waves, higher sea levels, and more severe droughts, wildfires, and downpours. Business resilience means assessing and managing these impacts on a company's facilities, operations, supply, and distribution chains, as well as costs.

Extreme weather can also keep employees from getting to work, disrupt communication systems, and threaten the availability of power and water supplies. However, there are also business opportunities to become more resilient. Some companies are already working on drought-resistant crops, storm-resistant building materials, and weather-related insurance products. Being prepared leverages business continuity and disaster recovery principles to help the company create a comprehensive natural disaster preparedness program. It includes everything from the greatest risks to how to plan and prepare, the best practices for recovery, and pivotal lessons learned from past disasters. See Figure 83 for types of weather disruptions.

Purpose. The purpose of this chapter is to describe how a weather disruption can impact business operations. The discussion is to assist in learning about the weather hazards that may strike your business and community, realizing the risks the company faces from weather disruptions and the local community's plans for warning and evacuation. The organization can augment this information by contacting the local government agencies at the federal and state levels.

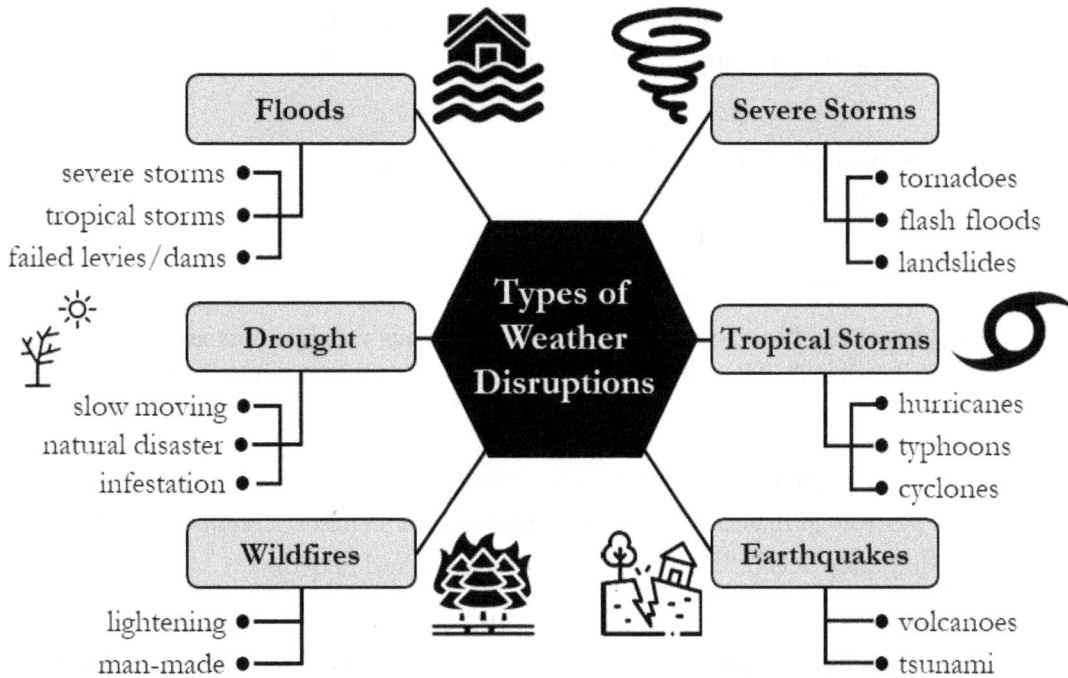

Figure 83: Many Types of Weather that Cause Disruptions

Challenge. Since most disruptions are unpredictable, the best way to prepare for severe weather is to anticipate the harsh circumstances that can arise from one. The challenge is to prepare by creating possible scenarios, developing a weather disruption plan, and allocating early warning alerts and signals. Know the location of available resources, personnel, and safety equipment and how to contact first responders.

Description. Planning is fundamentally a process to manage risk. Figure 84 provides the five major elements of a Disruption Preparedness Plan for a weather disruption or natural disaster.

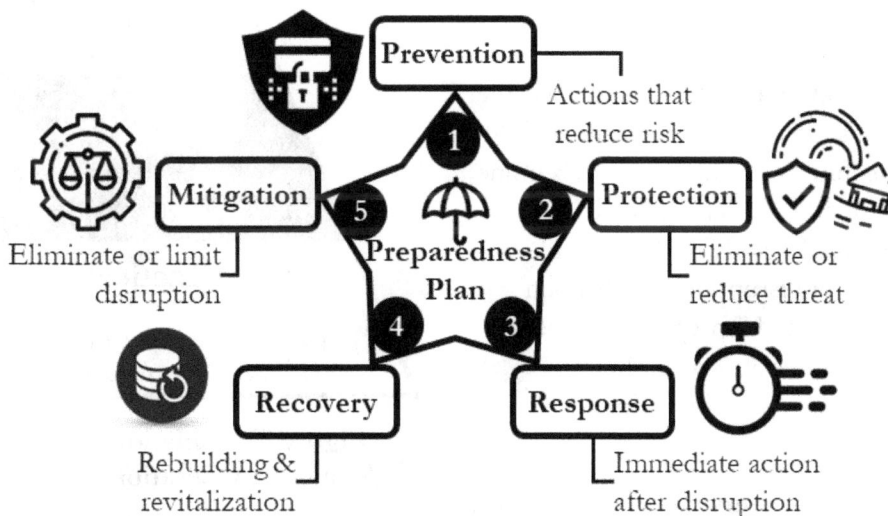

Figure 84: Elements of the Preparedness Plan

Perform a weather disruption risk assessment. Estimate the likelihood of severe weather events and evaluate the risks and their impact on the organization's critical business functions. Consider the following:

1. Damage to Assets and Physical Property
2. Damage to Raw Materials
3. Supply Chain Disruptions
4. Workers are Unable to Do Their Job

Identify critical business functions. The essential functions of a business are activities that are vital to a company's survival. These functions are susceptible to downtime. In addition, think about:

- Fulfilling legal or financial obligations to maintain cash flow.
- Playing a key role in maintaining the business' market share or reputation.
- Safeguarding irreplaceable assets such as IT systems and networks.

Develop an emergency action section as part of the weather disruption plan. It should clearly define the weather disruption team's roles, responsibilities, and activities. This plan should include up-to-date contact information, emergency contacts, a transparent chain of command, evacuation and contingency procedures, and step-by-step instructions to ensure the safety of employees and recovery of critical business functions. There are three tiers of planning: strategic planning, operational planning, and tactical (incident scene) planning. See Figure 85.

Communicate with all stakeholders inside and outside the organization. Often, employees and interested parties hear about a crisis during the disruption. It is best to develop consistent communications with employees, suppliers, leadership, and the community as part of the plan. They need to know what to expect and understand the recovery plan before events occur.

Test and then test again. Practice the weather disruption plan, simulate a severe weather event, and act out the initial response phase. Examine the results for significant details, defective communications links, and limited available resources. Weather disruptions can happen anywhere, at any time. Unprepared companies suffer the most significant losses. Being proactive helps employees react without panicking.

Improve disaster recovery. Recovery is never a simple task; two suggestions are listed below.

Figure 85: Relationship between Strategic, Operational, & Tactical Planning

1. **Leverage technology.** There are many technology solutions for disaster recovery. Tailor available applications and tools to the business, assets, location, and workforce.
2. **Ensure everything is documented.** Insurance can be an effective risk management tool to help companies bounce back after a disruption. Businesses need to prove claims and gain greater insight into how to improve resilience in the future.

Communicate across all business units. This includes the workforce, insurance agents, suppliers, first responders, third parties, and the community. The aftermath is an important period. Dialogues are critical to executing recovery efforts. Failure to coordinate could leave people with an incomplete picture of what happened and why.

Solution. The suggestions below and those shown in Figure 86 provide a framework for an organization's actions to develop a weather disruption plan and prepare the company workforce and workplace for surviving a possible disaster.

Build awareness. Build a common understanding of the physical risks associated with extreme weather and climate change and their potential impacts on a wide range of business activities. Building a credible business case requires a foundation of understanding about possible risks.

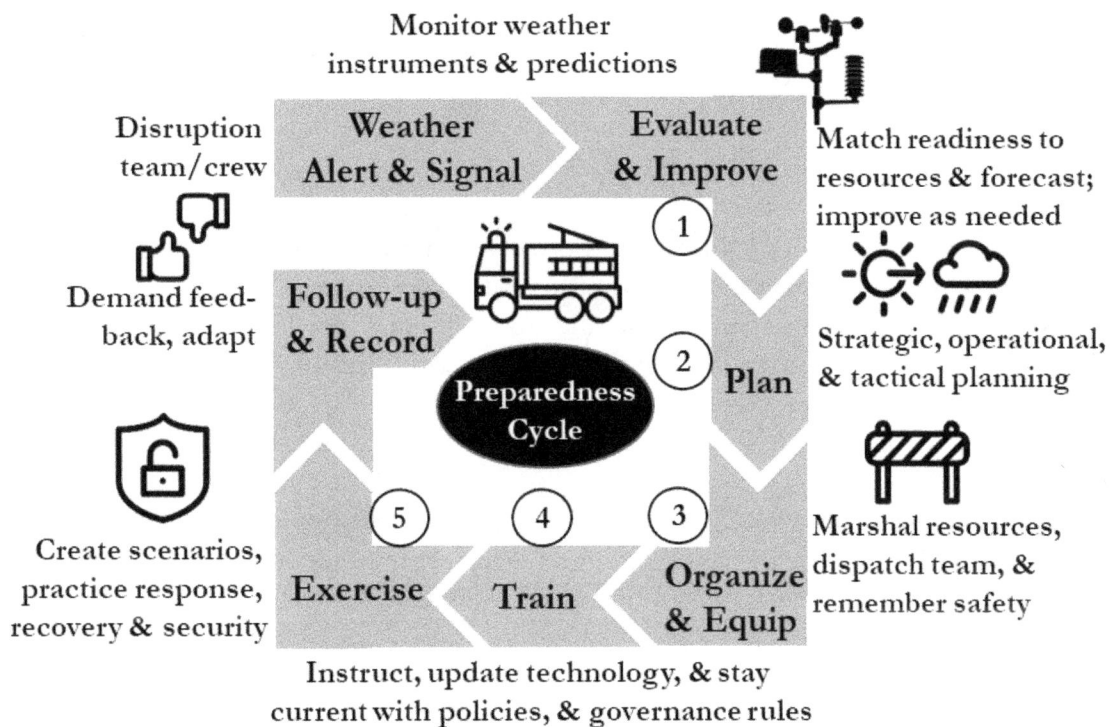

Figure 86: Suggested Steps in Preparing for a Weather Disruption

Assess vulnerabilities. Expand risk assessments to identify the extent to which recent weather extremes have adversely impacted facilities and operations and the impacts that future changes in the risks of such events could have. Past indicators, current trends, and future climate change projections must be considered.

Manage risks. Organizations build greater resilience beyond standard practice or standard engineering design criteria that are not based on a single factor but rather balance several considerations. Suggestions to manage risks are provided below:

- Fortifying or relocating infrastructure and facilities
- Managing risk within supply chains
- Overseeing or adjusting insurance coverage

Pursue opportunities. Develop plans to prioritize response actions and maximize opportunities associated with a changing climate. For example, serve new demands for existing products, improve efficiency, reduce costs, and develop new products and services.

Assessment and review. By incorporating the risks of physical impacts into ongoing risk management activities, risks and responses are periodically updated as new information becomes available.

Summary. The weather affects consumers' behavior regarding what products they buy, where they buy them, and in what quantity. Even if a business knows how normal weather affects its earnings, unexpected abnormal severe weather disruptions present their risks, and the organization may not be able to return in the same manner.

References & Bibliography.

1. Jean-Louis Bertrand and Miia Parnaudeau, "Severe Weather Threatens Businesses. It's Time to Measure and Disclose the Risks," Harvard Business Review; September 14, 2017
2. Sara Kendall, "How Business Can Weather the Storm," Center for Climate and Energy Solutions Center for Climate and Energy Solutions; January 19, 2014
3. "3 Ways Winter Weather Can Disrupt Business Continuity," Agility; December 12, 2019
4. Diana Olick, "Climate change supply chain disruptions: How to prepare," CNBC August 19, 2021
5. "Business continuity: Managing disaster and disruption," Allianz; September 2, 2017
6. "Natural Disaster Response and Recovery," U.S. Department of the Interior; 2022
7. "Disaster Preparedness, Response, and Recovery," Substance Abuse and Mental Health Services Administration (SAMHSA); 2022
8. "How To Create A Natural Disaster Preparedness Plan," Resolver; 2022
9. "National Disaster Recovery Framework," FEMA; 2022
10. "Basic Preparedness Planning," FEMA; 2022
11. "Comprehensive Preparedness Guide Developing And Maintaining Emergency Operations Plans," Department of Homeland Security; 2010
12. "Types of Disasters," SAMHSA; April 14, 2022
13. Meg Crawford and Stephen Seidel, "Weathering the Storm: Building Business Resilience to Climate Change," Center for Climate and Energy Solutions; 2013

Category: And two to grow on!
Truth #22. You will face legal issues.

Background & Introduction. During this unprecedented uncertainty and turmoil in the capital markets, supply chains, service industries, retail world, health industry, travel industry, and overall business environment, there is no "business as usual." Of all the causes of disruption discussed in this volume, the most volatile is the topic of business legal issues. The organization can be destroyed with one misstep, and the penalties can be devastating. The adages shown in Figure 87 state the two ruling adages regarding legal issues disruption.

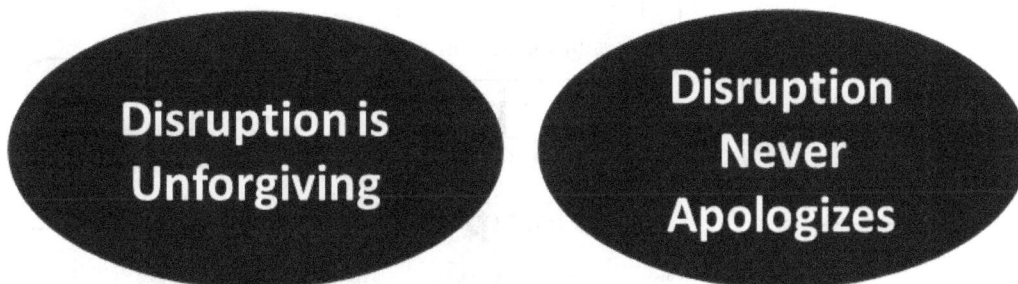

Figure 87: Disruption Adages that Apply to Legal Issues

Purpose. This chapter aims to highlight the role that legal issues can exacerbate disruption by multiplying the effect caused by other disruptions. The legal issues disruption results can result in permanent organization suffering. This can be realized in fines, legal restrictions, production area denial, and/or something more substantial from federal law enforcement or just public perception. Many business disruptions involve the supply chain because there are many players and moving parts. This chapter uses a hypothetical example of a supply chain failure that can develop into a disruption quickly.

Challenges. One day, a customer uses the company's products and is seriously injured. That injured party files a lawsuit. During the investigation, it was determined that the product was incorrectly manufactured by one of the suppliers. This occurred because the supplier couldn't meet the demand based on the approved design and cut some corners. This developed into a class action suit, law enforcement got involved, and a legal issue disruption was born.

A strategic approach to political risk management is needed immediately. As argued in previous chapters, disruption can be a massive opportunity. The organization must view and adopt those moments when disruption serendipity breaks in their favor. This example may not be an opportunity yet, but it must be mitigated immediately. As often happens, the coverup can be worse than the mishap.

Solution. The solution for legal issues causing disruption follows similar principles from the previous chapters. Your organization must have a disruption plan identifying the personnel and resources available to mitigate disruption effects. Every possibility will not be foreseen, but prepare as well as possible. The legal issue disruption category is very disparate and diverse. The disruption team must ensure that a tiny disruption doesn't beget more, and then a snowball effect results. The description below highlights some of the probable representative legal issues to consider when preparing for this type of disruption.

Description. Business owners in the U.S. are often faced with various legal problems that can be crippling to their business. One of the best ways to circumvent these legal problems is to identify potential problem areas early and prepare for them by having an effective disruption team in place. This often includes an executive, lawyer, investigator, and action plan. Figure 88 illustrates nine potential legal problems.

Figure 88: Legal Issues Examples that may Cause Disruption

1. **Business structure.** Every business needs to start on the right footing, including the company's structure. The wrong business structure for your type of business can have severe tax and legal consequences.

2. **Employee and partnership agreements.** One of the most common legal problems is "wrongful termination" claims made by employees. Contracts are essential when hiring employees because word of mouth and handshakes are not considered binding. The same principles apply to partnership agreements when adding and subtracting partners.

3. **Employee misclassification.** The Federal Department of Labor requires employees to be correctly classified. This can impact insurance and worker's compensation payments.

4. **They have dissatisfied customer lawsuits.** Businesses can avoid issues with dissatisfied customers by taking a hands-on approach and addressing issues as soon as they arise.

5. **Disputes with suppliers, contractors, and competitors.** This can be a broad topic; however, improving communications with your subcontractors in your supply chain is very important to signal problems arising from this legal area.

6. **Tax and regulatory problems.** Taxes from many sources fall into this category. A few of them include income, social security withholding, sales, environment, property, and company taxes at the federal, state, and municipal levels. In addition, regulatory changes may impact your company's core competency. See Figure 89.

7. **Harassment and discrimination cases.** Your company needs to be prepared for this legal issue because swift action is usually required to get out in front of this disruption.

8. **Licenses and permits.** Registering for the correct licenses and permits allows you to operate your business and gives the company legal standing.

9. **Copyrights, patents, and trademarks.** Securing your intellectual property rights requires you to discover, document, and register inventions and ideas, but making that investment now will pay off significantly.

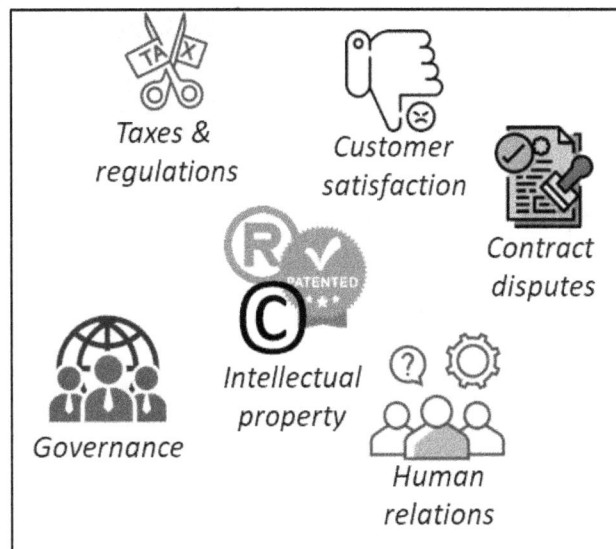

Figure 89: Legal Issues Impacting Disruption

Actions. An action plan is a checklist of the steps or tasks you must complete to achieve the company's goals and objectives. It's an essential part of strategic planning and helps improve disruption planning. See Figure 90.

Assign a legal disruption person in charge. This single person is responsible for forming a response to legal issue disruptions. The leader welcomes members from many company departments. The focus is on monitoring, recording, and trending legal issues as they occur.

Designate legal team members. The leader assigns tasks to a group of subject matter experts on the company's products, employees, supply chain, sales, public relations, and legal team. The team considers various scenarios germane to the company's core competency, looks for weaknesses and strengths, exercises the virtual response to scenarios, measures readiness, and predicts outcomes.

Provide a role for a public relations officer. Communicate often with the PR office to shape the company's face to the public and the government for the media during the disruption mitigation. Getting out in front of any issue usually ends in the best results.

Prepare legal issue disruption approach. The leader and their legal disruption team create an action plan, provide resources, and know their location and availability when needed to mitigate a disruption response.

Identify legal red flags and how those alerts present themselves. Open communication lines between the disruption team and other internal and external reporting agencies. Count events and know thresholds for customer complaints, safety accidents, supply chain disturbances, pricing issues, and legal notices. Ensure that the disturbance team is on distribution for these occurrences.

Capture legal data, contact information, legal climate, and precedence. Study previous instances from similar organizations. Know what has worked and, more importantly, what has not. This database becomes increasingly valuable the longer it exists. The database becomes critical for the next four action items. The next four action items apply to the information gathered in the database.

- **Evaluate, rethink, and target risky legal areas.**
- **Stay vigilant, sustain resources, and keep lines of communication open.**
- **Document mitigation lessons learned & record all results.**
- **Create a dashboard to display events related to legal issues and analyze trends.**

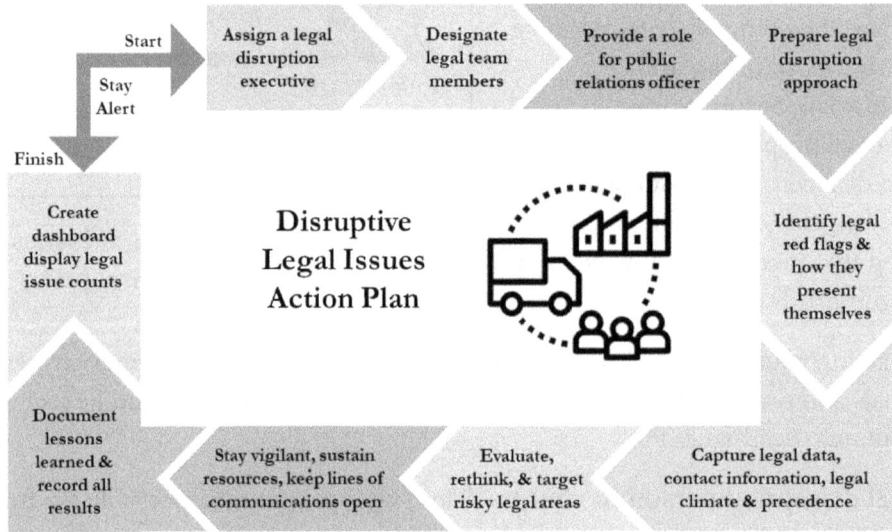

Figure 90: Suggested Actions for Legal Issue Disruption Preparation

Summary.

Legal disruptions can significantly impact businesses, economies, and societies. They often need more certainty, leading to delays in decision-making and increased costs as organizations navigate new regulations or legal challenges. Companies may face litigation, penalties, and reputational damage, while industries may experience shifts in competitive dynamics. Legal disruptions can spur innovation as businesses adapt to new legal landscapes, potentially leading to improved practices and products. On a broader scale, they can influence public policy and societal norms, driving changes in behavior and expectations among individuals and institutions.

References & Bibliography.

1. "When Business Blows Up Policy: How to Regulate Disruptions," Knowledge at Wharton; July 27, 2018
2. Teresa Paul, "Business Disruption Strategies," Hanson Bridgett; 2022
3. Courtney Rickert McCaffrey "When political disruption surrounds you, what's your next strategic move," EY-Building a Better Working World; May 26, 2022
4. "Supply Chain Disruption & How to Respond," Accenture; 2022
5. Jacob Maslaw, "7 Most Common Legal Problems Businesses Face in Their Operations," LegalScoops; August 22, 2020

Category: *Two to Grow On*

Truth #23. The future will not turn out as planned.

Background & Introduction. We can all use artificial intelligence to read the cosmos and alert us that disruption is nigh. It seems like danger, disguised as disruption, is all around us. Disruption becomes dangerous when we are not prepared, when we lose perspective, and when we fail to perform. We mitigate the threat by opening our minds to the potential of transformation.

Disruption isn't the antagonist when we change our viewpoint; it's an opportunity. Here is where innovation can produce tangible progress. How can I be ready for every contingency? Impossible, you say. Research shows us several examples of both successful and devastating disruptions. There are several actions that one can execute ahead of time to prepare.

Successful governance in today's fast-moving, global environment requires nurturing creative, flexible, and spirited managers who can effectively steer their organization through the current crisis while positioning it to thrive during the next one.

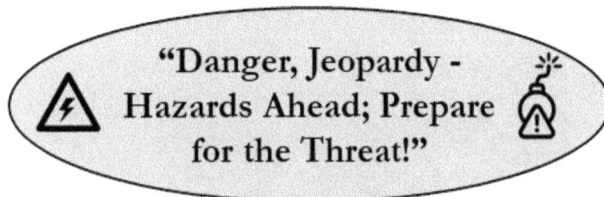

Figure 91: Disruption Peril Quote

Although it may be improbable to predict the next disturbance with certainty, the prepared leader assumes that disruption is inescapable. See Figure 91. It's like death and taxes; disruption is inevitable.

Purpose. This chapter aims to close out the disruption discussion by examining this topic in general for all situations. We will focus on the subject inherent in the quote below.

"We don't overcome change by being stronger or smarter than our competitors, but by being better able to adapt to it." Mike Ross, 2022

Challenge. Humans are inconsistent, sensitive, and passionate, making events and disruptions hard to forecast. Predicting any event's precise future impact and several other outcomes is challenging. When thinking about the future, we often overemphasize the role of technology and underestimate where technology fits in the business culture and societal tolerances.

Disruption has been studied for some time, and one of the conclusions is shown in Figure 92. Therefore, gambling is popular; we want to put a percentage on everything. Like a bookie, the successful executive does their homework, analyzes data, reads the signals, and is familiar with past performance. Add some luck, and voila, decide on risk/reward.

The leader is not only ready for disruption but also designs a response when it occurs. Success also requires impeccable judgment. This is the challenge presented by "the future will not turn out as planned because of disruption."

Figure 92: Disruption isn't Just an Extension of the Past

Description. Disruption survival is all about resiliency. Bouncing back from a severe blow to your business could be an opportunity to carve out a new market share or innovative product. Utilizing a collaborative platform by bringing buyers, suppliers, and other trading partners together helps businesses improve resiliency, mitigate possible risks, and optimize opportunities.

We plan in the perfect world but execute in the real world. But we must perform in this environment. We need the ability to transform quickly from Plan A to Plan B-Z. Many forces lead a business to disruption. See Figure 93 for a few nominations.

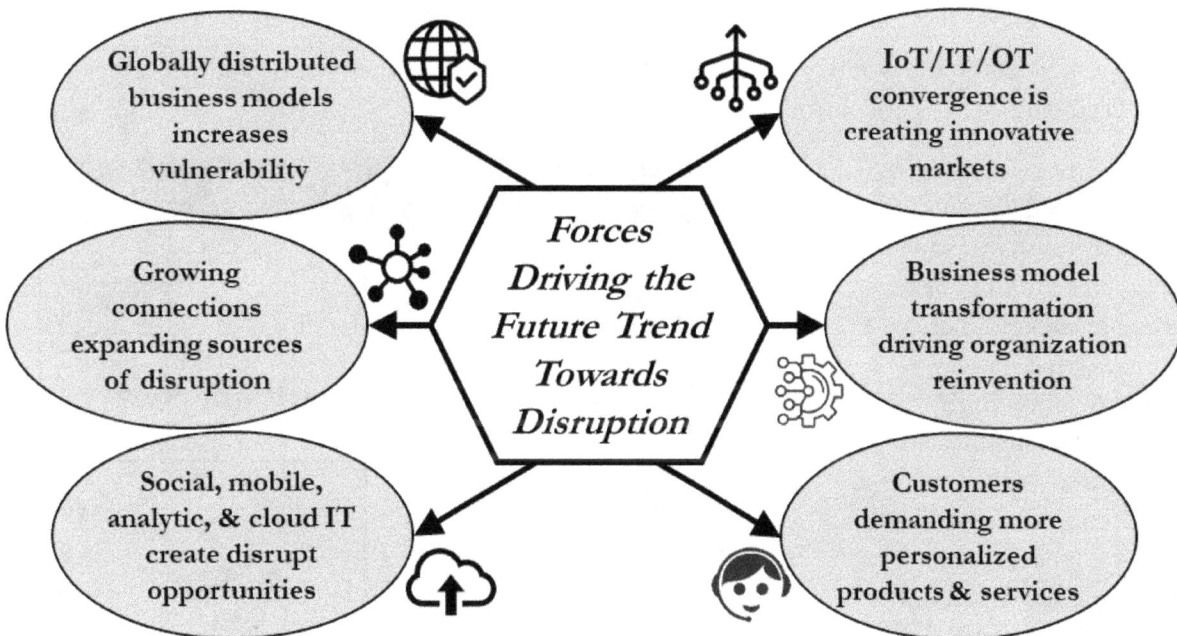

Figure 93: Forces that Drive the Future to Disruption

Companies that embrace the opportunity posed by disruption will need a new approach—one rooted in hope rather than fear and focused on the edge rather than the core. The patterns can help shape and clarify the opportunity. They can also help target efforts to strengthen the core business, maintaining the revenue stream to fund transformation while identifying where those efforts are misguided.

The list below provides four disruption opportunity approaches business leaders can use to realize disruption immediately.

1. Monitor the changes in the environment to identify genuinely disruptive happenings.
2. Revisit strategy for agility, adaptability, & responsiveness to emerging threats.
3. Employ IoT/AR/ML analysis tools & techniques to cope with risk at higher levels of sophistication.
4. Recognize organizational blind spots, built-in institutional challenges, & personal biases.

Businesses still need help deciding which path to follow, taking a risk on innovation, or sticking with what the company already does well.

Solution. The following suggestions are offered for consideration as you prepare for disruption.

Get clarity, the wisdom of preparation. The wisest among us know how to use this current disruption in your business as an honest assessment. Otherwise, you have squandered a golden opportunity.

Create a disruption plan as part of your business plan. Make a daily appointment with your plan. Reviewing your business plan daily is a non-negotiable step for success. Give yourself the earliest opportunity to correct the course as the landscape transforms. See Figure 94.

Place markers out in the world (you define the scope) that you can check daily and will appear on your dashboard (whatever control panel you use).

These human alert sensors need to be a diverse lot. They should span a wide geographic area and be of disparate backgrounds. The industrial sensors should be of multiple technologies and located throughout your supply and distribution chains. Plus, it connects to all aspects of the media, both social and traditional. Look for red flags, recognize a problem area, and open communication lines.

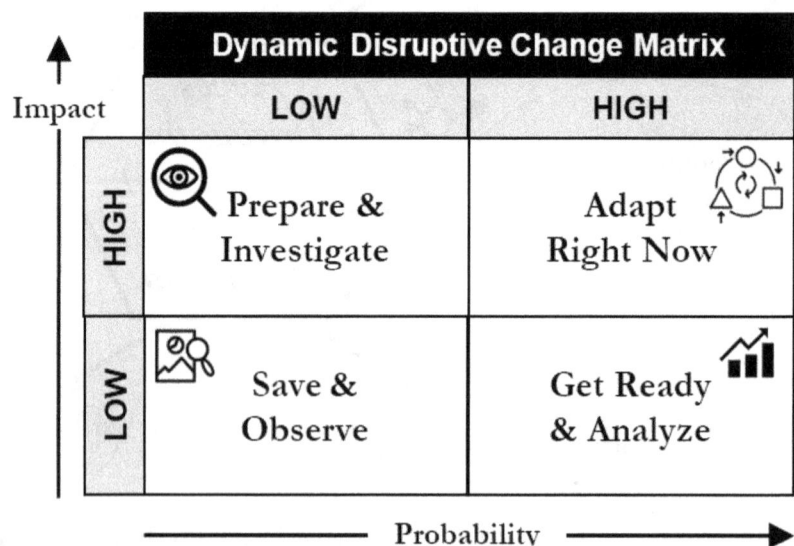

Figure 94: Dynamic Disruptive Change Matrix

Dynamic Disruptive Change Matrix		
Impact	LOW	HIGH
HIGH	Prepare & Investigate	Adapt Right Now
LOW	Save & Observe	Get Ready & Analyze

Probability →

Make this an early warning system.

Seek out disruption-tolerant operations to produce your goods and services. For example, if you have one supplier for a vital product component, you should perform due diligence on having a backup in place. Now, expand that argument to your entire operation. Record all this information for training, completeness, and review.

Flexibility and agility are required. The best leaders are agile and work on their skills with practice. That's correct; practice disruption. Utilize your best analytic tools, adopt artificial intelligence, run various scenarios, and storyboard what-if situations. The best athletes and minds do this to achieve their best and avoid injury.

Focus on training and keeping a multi-skilled workforce. With automation happening so quickly, society can only reliably predict what skills will be needed a few years later. We will only have trained people how to code; for example, AI can perform basic coding.

None of us is a seer, and disruption planning is not about knowing what will happen in the future. It is about preparing yourself when something goes wrong. Whether it is a bad actor, a new competitor, a global pandemic, a world disaster, a climate event, or technological advancement, disruption will arrive at your doorstep. The only unknown is when.

We conclude by taking one upcoming disruption in detail to portend a future business climate that may be totally different from today's business climate. Here are example areas in which the arrival of *artificial intelligence* may disrupt operations horizontally and vertically:

Automation of Tasks: AI can automate repetitive tasks across various departments, reducing the need for manual labor and increasing operational efficiency. This can include tasks like data entry, customer service inquiries, and routine decision-making processes.

Data Analysis and Insights: AI-powered analytics can process vast amounts of data at high speeds to extract actionable insights and trends. Businesses can use this information to optimize strategies, improve decision-making, and identify new growth opportunities.

Personalized Customer Experiences: AI algorithms can analyze customer data to personalize marketing messages, recommend products or services, and tailor interactions based on individual preferences and behavior. This leads to improved customer satisfaction and loyalty.

Predictive Maintenance: AI-enabled predictive maintenance systems can analyze equipment data to anticipate when machinery or systems will likely fail. By detecting issues early, businesses can schedule maintenance proactively, minimize downtime, and reduce maintenance costs.

Supply Chain Optimization: AI algorithms can optimize supply chain operations by predicting demand, optimizing inventory levels, and identifying the most efficient transportation routes. This leads to reduced costs, improved delivery times, and better inventory management.

Fraud Detection and Prevention: AI-powered fraud detection systems can analyze patterns and anomalies in financial transactions, helping businesses identify and prevent fraudulent activities in real time.

Natural Language Processing (NLP): NLP technology enables machines to understand and generate human language, facilitating applications such as chatbots for customer service, sentiment analysis of social media data, and language translation services.

Healthcare Diagnostics and Treatment: In the healthcare industry, AI can analyze medical images, genetic data, and patient records to assist with diagnosis, treatment planning, and drug discovery, potentially leading to more accurate diagnoses and personalized treatment options.

Financial Trading: AI algorithms can analyze market data, news, and other relevant factors to make rapid trading decisions. High-frequency trading firms use AI to execute trades at speeds and frequencies beyond human capability, potentially disrupting traditional trading strategies.

Creative Content Generation: AI tools can generate content such as articles, music, or artwork based on algorithms trained on large datasets. While still in its early stages, this technology could disrupt journalism, entertainment, and marketing industries.

Workforce Transformation: AI may change the nature of work by augmenting human capabilities and creating new job roles while transforming existing ones. Businesses need to adapt their workforce skills and structures to leverage AI effectively.

Ethical and Regulatory Considerations: The adoption of AI raises ethical and regulatory challenges related to data privacy, algorithm bias, job displacement, and accountability for AI-driven decisions. Businesses must navigate these issues to ensure responsible and ethical AI deployment.

Summary. Strategic planning experts note the value of imagining different scenarios and their impact on a long-term strategic plan is in the process, not the details. In other words, successfully planning for the next disruption is about more than predicting exactly what that disruption will look like. Instead, it's about identifying organizational strengths and weaknesses and cultivating a leadership structure that can think creatively about a variety of contingency plans.

References & Bibliography.

1. Deirdre Sartorelli and James L. Kawski, "Three Ways to Make Disruption Become an Inflection Point for Opportunity," June 26, 2020
2. Brandvoice, "The Importance of Planning in A Year of Disruption and Reimagination," Innovation; May 31, 2021
3. Tam Harbert, "Technology and the Future of Work: Which Way Will We Go?" SHRM; July 24, 2022
4. "Planning for Tomorrow's Disruption - Professional Development," Harvard DCE; July 24, 2022
5. Linda Lacina, "How to weather a potential downturn – and compassion's role," World Economic Forum; July 19, 2022
6. John Seely Brown, "Approaching disruption: Charting a course for new growth and performance at the edge and beyond," Deloitte Insights; October 5, 2015
7. Mike Ross, "Prepare your business for future disruption," BDC CEO Excellence Retreat; 2022
8. Katie Malone, "7 digital disruptions reshaping business by 2025," CIO Dive; October 27, 2020
9. Nancy Albinson, "Trend 9 _ Business Disruption Risk – Future of Risk," Deloitte US; 2022
10. "15 Technologies That Will Disrupt the Industry In The Next Five Years," Forbes Technology Council; May 7, 2020
11. "Business disruption: everything you need to know," Robbins; 2022
12. "Persistent Forecasting of Disruptive Technologies," Committee on Forecasting Future Disruptive Technologies; 2015
13. Discover the AI-Powered Future: Understanding AIC Hours of Operation and Working Hours for Seamless Integration - Opening Hours Today. https://openinghourstoday.com/aic-hours/

www.ingramcontent.com/pod-product-compliance
Lightning Source LLC
Chambersburg PA
CBHW062028210326

41519CB00060B/7198